Self-Respect
The Solution to Unsolvable Problems
Martin Tomback

Self-Respect: The Solution to Unsolvable Problems

Martin Tomback

Published by Martin Tomback, 2024.

While every precaution has been taken in the preparation of this book, the publisher assumes no responsibility for errors or omissions, or for damages resulting from the use of the information contained herein.

SELF-RESPECT: THE SOLUTION TO UNSOLVABLE PROBLEMS

First edition. August 19, 2024.

Copyright © 2024 Martin Tomback.

ISBN: 978-0975524879

Written by Martin Tomback.

Whatever games are played with us, we must play no games with ourselves, but deal in our privacy with the last honesty and truth.

-Ralph Waldo Emerson, Illusions, The Atlantic, November 1857

Contents

The Author
Introduction
Chapter 1 - Your Personal Environment 1
Chapter 2 - Self-Love 21
Chapter 3 - Free Expression 41
Chapter 4 - Survival 57
Chapter 5 - Your success is in *you*. 71
Chapter 6 - Self Talk 83
Chapter 7 - Confidence 97
Chapter 8 - There's nothing wrong with you. 109
Chapter 9 - You, Your Soul, & I 123
Chapter 10 - If you were God, what would you . do differently? 135
Chapter 11 - Motivation 147

The Author

What's the first thing you should ask a genius? "What are you good at?" of course. Geniuses have their own talents and predilections. They're not all the same. They excel at particular things. If you asked me, I'd have to say, "God stuff." Of all the unlikely things, I'm comfortable talking about God. It comes naturally to me. I understand it. There's not much money in it, but it's always interesting. And there are plenty of interesting types floating around ready to help me. Now it gets weird. I think I'm friends with God. It's not simply that God loves everyone. Certainly that's true. I literally believe God and I are friends, pals. It's really not much of a stretch. It's a universal concept so why shouldn't God have friends too? God does and I'm one of them. Yes, it comes with perks and it also comes with responsibilities, like any friends. God never says "no" to me, and I never say "no" to God. We keep an eye on each other. We share our problems. And, as you would expect, one way or another, things always work out.

I spent my whole life observing human nature. It came easily to me. Life was confusing and I wanted to know what I was doing. I wanted to be successful. I wanted things, and I wanted to feel good about myself. I wanted answers that made sense. I wanted to understand it all. And I wanted dependable values I could trust. What's right and what's wrong? It's a life's work for everyone. I discovered amazing things. But it didn't get the attention I expected. I thought I had a mission from God and I wanted to share what I learned. I've come to accept God has its own way of doing things. I like writing. It's relaxing. I drift off into a trance, deep in contemplation. I feel like an inventor crafting familiar parts into brand new things. It's a puzzle. The mechanism is words. When it feels right they have a cadence, a rhythm, that I hope makes it comfortable for the reader to understand. It lets me turn my soul's insights into something worthwhile I can share.

Writing made me. I'm more sympathetic when I write. I'm really a misfit, a bit of a hermit. I don't feel connected to the mass consciousness. That gives me the freedom to question everything. I identify with many things but I'm not attached to anything. Everything has to prove itself. I want the truth beyond anyone's opinion. I want to know what God wants. Call it maturity or a blessing, but it's comforting to get away from life's struggles and find solace in God's compassion. So I live my life as a prayer with my eyes always on God. It's good luck. And I get plenty of help from spirit. Problems are puzzles and burdens become exercise. And I know exactly who to blame for my problems. I complain all the time but I never feel abandoned. The respect I had for myself in my early successes became the maturity I know today. It's an endless process of ups and downs and making the best of it. The goals I chased were sincere but mere distractions next to the Love that built my character. Love is the Divine Consciousness. It's not another sentiment. It's the common sense in God's Creation. It's wise that I trusted it because it worked...and nothing else did.

Introduction

The challenge for self-respect is finding a fair balance. It has to be comfortable. It's your respect for your responsibility to what life has for you. Finding the right balance is the solution to everything.

Life may not be what you wanted. Fortunately, you have self-respect to help you. It helps create your attitude. It's how you accommodate your values. Self-respect is always positive. If you find yourself with a negative thought, it's your attitude that needs to change. Sometimes all you can do is wait till things get better. Nature may not accept your idea of what's right at the moment. It often has to be coaxed. You make adjustments and Nature responds. That's how you find a compromise. That's how you find your balance. Like an old radio, you have to go back and forth before you get a clear signal. Life is like that radio. There's a lot to consider and you have to tune it in to get a pleasing sound.

As disastrous as a situation is, suffering makes it a problem. So don't suffer. Easy to say, but it's also easier than hopelessness. If every day was a peaceful Sunday you'd make better choices. Wisdom surfaces when you're at peace with yourself. More likely, life requires your attention when you're anxious and confused. Necessity energizes your self-respect no matter how bewildered you are. Think how fast you react to an errant driver. It may not be a cascade of self-respect but it's enough to keep you alive. Self-preservation is instinctive. Self-respect is your choice.

Every day you try to avoid problems. Self-respect guides you to make the right choices. Positive thoughts focus on doing better. Self-respect embraces that intent. It makes you stronger. You're more confident when you're stronger. Weakness makes it easy to feel sorry for yourself. It's frustrating. It takes patience to stick with something till you have what you want. Making a good decision is easier when you're strong. You enjoy the confidence in your ability. What's hard is doing your best when you're weak. It's no fault to fail when you do your best. When you're sincere, you do the work and hope for a good result. But the question is always, "Could you have done better?" Success is an honest answer, not finding an excuse.

Self-respect is learned. You learn to align your opinion with a positive attitude. Positive thinking inspires your courage. It teaches you to stand up for your values. Everything has a purpose. There's no pain without a purpose. Pain forces you to focus on how to feel good. You want to end the pain and make sure it doesn't happen again. You have to love yourself. You can't have a positive thought without loving yourself. You can be wrong as long as you're honest. Self-respect respects your honesty. It's Love's test. To pass the spiritual test you must pass the social test. Your soul is good at it. You have free will and you have imagination. That's more than enough to do whatever you want.

Every thought you have questions your self-respect. Every moment is a balance of self-respect and respect for your environment, including everyone in it. It's the starting point for your relationships. It's how you communicate your values. It's your creativity making the choices you hope are good for you. Self-respect doesn't depend on someone else respecting you. Being respected matters but it comes with responsibilities. You have to accept the consequences of your actions and how they affect others. In the shared morality in every relationship, mutual respect is the foundation for compromise. It's social maturity. You want it to be fair because you want to be treated fairly. Creating social formulas that everyone can accept is the challenge. Fairness creates the opportunity for everyone to include their perspective. Everyone bargains so everyone can win.

Self-respect is your responsibility. You're the only one who can do it. Maybe you need help, but even then you're responsible for getting help. Your mind processes everything, but you decide where to begin and where to end. It has to be acceptable to you because you decide your values. You might be married for 60 years or divorce in 6 months. Every situation has a different lesson. Society has its rules and you have yours. Society serves society and you have to serve yourself. You can enjoy your self-respect no matter where you are in life's hierarchy because you always have the option to do something else. How you see yourself has little to do with how others see you. You have a responsibility to your job because that's how you make money to pay your bills. But there's no priority in one person's self-respect over another's or any justification for it. You do your best with what you have. Relationships have personal goals and if it takes working on someone else's, fit in where you can and enjoy the benefit whether it's a raise in pay or a good night kiss. Whatever it is, make yourself worth it. That you can control.

Problems don't relate to self-respect. Problems relate to achieving a goal. Self-respect is being confident you'll succeed with your values intact. Unsolvable problems are solved by being confident. Results, who knows? Be sincere and hope for the best. Evaluate the result then revise your plan or revise your attitude. That's the solution to life; identify the problem, ask good questions, act with a purpose, and let Love guide you. As long as you're sincere, God's plan is the problem and you can't do much about it except get on board. As illogical as it sounds, the physical world is inconsequential beyond that.

So what's the world telling you? What does society value? Is it having a sports car you'll never drive fast or a gorgeous dress you'll only wear once? Is it a fabulous vista on the other side of the world or the recipe for a fattening pastry? You might want to be president but are you prepared to murder thousands of people? Many people spend years training for professions to find they really don't like the job. It's the paradox of marvelous things. It's different how you admire something compared to the actual experience. You might like that you've done it, but would you do it again? Was it everything you expected? Was it wishful thinking or your divine purpose? It matters because it comes from your opinion. Whatever it is, it's your right to choose it.

You want answers. You want to experience everything. You want to see for yourself. You want the adventure and thrill of discovery. You may dream of traveling around the world but do you exploit your current opportunities? Do you visit your local museums? Do you try something different for dinner? Is the next new thing the "be-all, end-all" or "been there, done that?" It's easy to get bored. You're designed to solve mysteries. When you can't find one; you take a drink, watch TV, or find another distraction. With all life's opportunities, people just want to hide. It's because people have limits. Life is the process of limits.

The problem is immaturity. Life is for developing sensible values. The adventure is always there but you have to mature into it. It takes time. Self-respect supports your ambition. It's easy to get lost. It's easy to get tired. Without relief, you can burn out. "I've had enough of this." you mutter to yourself. Then you turn it all off. You look for anything with the promise of Peace; quitting your job, binging on brownies, or some thoughtless romance. But the wrong distraction can ruin you. You can wind up broke, fat, and alone. Life's confusing. There are too many options. You still want to do well. You want to care about people. But everyone has a different point of view. The good news is there's one value you can always count on, Love. Love is always the right choice. Your challenge is the way you characterize it.

You have to energize yourself. Take a nap. Exercise. Listen to music. But *do something*. You need relief. Exhaustion can fool you into thinking you're out of ideas, that you've lost your fascination with life. But re-energized, it's easy to refocus your attention. You have a responsibility. You have the world to command. It could be as easy as a change of style to invigorate your old routine, like a new pair of shoes. But you have to want it. You have to encourage it. You have to trust your self-respect will give it to you.

Trust your ability. It's not a skill or talent. It's your belief in yourself. It's your confidence. That's your biggest asset. It's like your workout partner saying, "One more time. You can do it." You feel your own support. It comes from God where there's no doubt about your purpose, only a question how you'll do it. You'll find a way. Success is the only road you have. It sounds funny with all the misery in the world but your success is guaranteed. Success is what you learn from your experience. It's your maturity. It's your sense that there's a perfect way to do it. It may not be society's way, but it's custom-made for you. The world will eventually come around.

Part of solving a problem is how fast you can do it. There's always the story of a six year old solving a Rubik's Cube in a five seconds while doing 360's on a skate board. It's because speed is one way we measure success. Like the winner of a marathon, it's definable who came in first. The rate your character matures is less definable. It's more like training for a marathon. It's measured by improvements. It's subjective because people value things differently. People come from different environments. Values change with the demands of their environment. Values mean it's your choice. Love is universal but its characteristics must accommodate you. Some things you'll like and some you won't. Everyone has to adapt. It's God's challenge how we love each other and respect each other's values. Confrontational personalities can be a problem. They test you even when you don't feel like being tested. You can only change yourself. You can't force someone to change their attitude. It depends on their rate of maturity no matter how long it takes. It depends on Love overcoming life's limits. It's more a direction than a result.

Quality is a level of achievement. It defines how close you are to your goal. You may want everything perfect at your wedding but you can wear old pajamas to take out the garbage. It's setting priorities for the conditions you'll accept. That's why designer labels are so popular. They symbolize quality, and that's often measured by the money they spend on advertising. You may not know exactly what you want so you need help to confirm it. You need that designer label. It represents a level of quality that's generally accepted. It means you have to be honest with yourself and have an idea of what you want. That designer shoe still has to be comfortable. All the envy in the world won't help you if your foot hurts. It doesn't matter if it's leather seats for your car or a hug from your kids. The important questions are, "Is this what you had your heart set on? Does this have the quality you wanted? Are you happy now?"

Sincerity is the essence of self-respect. It's being honest with yourself. You have to accept who you are; warts and all. You have to accept it on your own terms. You have to be brave enough to look at yourself in the mirror. Your reward is the truth. That's how you know you're not fooling yourself. How can you be sure you're not rationalizing away something important? How can you be sure what you want isn't following someone else's opinion? Is their advice good advice...for you? Sincerity is your protection. When you want what's right for you, you'll know when you have it. And you'll know what's wrong for you too.

The other issue is social. How do you get along with others? How does society define the limits of your self-respect? What's acceptable? What's required? What's intrusive? Are you living off the grid in Alaska or in a 25 story high-rise? Some people joke about their foibles and others see it as an insult. Many think their self-respect depends on what others think about them, like some Victorian judgment. It's the old story about who's popular and who's the outcast. It starts on the playground and ends in the boardroom, but it's the same game. Everyone wants to be included. It's the social average where everyone can be comfortable. The rules may limit you if you're a dreamer or protect you as you retreat into some acceptable irresponsibility, like drinking too much. Being included is the tightrope we all have to walk, from the lone-wolf biker to the second viola in the orchestra. That's what society is; sharing the benefits and responsibilities of being alive.

Tolerance challenges your self-respect. Everyone has their own way of doing things, but you have to respect your values. You have to know your limits. You learn to fine-tune your attitude to your different responsibilities. Problems are normal, then you're confronted by the hopelessness of someone suffering hardships more than anyone could handle. How should you respond? What serves your values? You have to trust Love. Love balances everything. Love puts your energy where it can do the most good. Then you have to figure out why. It's the consciousness of Creation, from a toddler's scribbles to the indecipherable writing on an ancient tomb. Love joins it together. Logic is the same everywhere. Physics is the same. It doesn't matter what language you speak. It doesn't matter what planet you're from. The same energy created everything. Your free will tests it. It's one big experiment with God endlessly muttering, "Yes. I thought so."

Revealing yourself can be scary. It's more than mindless gossip. It trusts someone with your honest thoughts and hopes you won't be judged. It depends on mutual respect. But how much can you trust a stranger? You watch them. You consider their reactions. You see each other at your best and understand what could bring out the worst. You express your values and consider theirs. You rely on your self-respect to know your trust is safe. A friend is a long-term commitment. It's a rare opportunity with a generous reward, finding a stranger who loves you for who you are. The greatest achievement in self-preservation is finding another soul who cares about you. Friends cooperate. It could mean helping you do something when they're tired from a long day's work. Friends share the effort. Friends share the benefit. Friends go out of their way for each other when the only success is the Love they share in friendship. Friends trust that their sacrifice benefits everyone. Friends won't let a doubt diminish their self-respect. They're honest about it. They won't shy away from the awkwardness in a relationship if they trust it. They'll talk about it. They'll look for a better balance. When you see the same person every day you're seeing the seeds of a friendship. There's an attraction. Whether it lives up to your expectations or dies in ignorance is up to you. Friendship is experienced through your soul. You like someone and they like you. You have the same outlook. Then you decide if you'll support it. The important thing is it's dependable. Whatever it becomes, it grows through your self-respect.

Self-respect shines in the social experience. It wants fairness in every relationship. It represents your responsibility to yourself plus your responsibility to everyone else. It's the basis for civilization solving the problems that keep everyone safe. It's the wisdom of working together. Reasonable voices share their hopes in how they want a problem solved. They often want different results but they all want the problem to end. Finding a formula that satisfies everyone is what reasonable people do. It's what a loving society does. You honor your self-respect by knowing how much you can compromise and still get what you want. You do it for yourself knowing everyone benefits. And it's the same for the person sitting next to you.

Self-respect compels you to find support. You need help. Everyone needs help. You need resources. You need experience. You need a pat on the back for encouragement. You need to know you're not alone, that there's someone to pick you up when you fall down. First, you have to trust yourself. Your self-respect won't leave you. It's impossible. You'll get lost from time to time. People have different schedules. You may extend yourself beyond your support or fall behind when the pace is too fast. But God doesn't rely on human plans. God has its own plan. Your course may change but you're always headed forward. You do what you think is best even when you're wrong. You keep improving and mature with every step. You get better with practice because practice means control.

You question everything because your attention is an investment in yourself. What seems like an unsolvable problem is often a matter of patience. Focus on the problem and the answer eventually comes; whether you think it's from God, intuitive analysis, or dumb luck. And you don't have to be smart. Universal intelligence is inseparable from your awareness. It's simply a matter of tapping into it once you free yourself from earthly concerns. You already know the answer. You just have to find it. "Out of the mouths of babes" really means "out of the mouth of universal consciousness." Trust your innocence and Love will show you the way.

You don't have to do anything special. Just do what you think will make things better. Self-respect comes naturally but its value is learned. Sometimes an unsolvable problem has no value so it never was a problem. It only mimicked one at the time. It was your opinion. Maturity means learning the value of things. Most people don't know so they follow the crowd. It doesn't take much effort. "They're doing it so I'll do it too. It must be good if everyone's doing it." Shared excitement is a common substitute for value but a thoughtless sentiment is hardly worth something as dear as a trusted friend. It's like gambling with the rent money. Some people take forever to learn it and some people just know. They were blessed with common sense or taught to care about others instead of playing with toys. It takes effort to question your values but not a big effort, just the intention to be honest with yourself. Few people know that. You're more likely to chase what's popular; some new style here today and gone tomorrow. Religion and philosophy fill the gap but they can't work without your support. It takes time to understand your relationships to the point you know what you want. It's your responsibility to choose an identity for your self-respect. You live most of your life with it so you want it to be right. It doesn't have to be some ascetic ritual where you deny yourself your pleasures. Enjoy yourself but have sensible limits. Bless yourself with right choices, at least in your sincerity.

Where's your responsibility? How do you value your self-respect? How do you tally the pros and cons? How do you define success? You want what you want whatever it is. You like it and you want to feel good about it. It's your right to feel good. Having what you want gives you a good opinion of yourself. But ask yourself, "Is it honesty or would you be dishonest to make an extra dollar? Do you have courage or would you make an excuse to avoid your fear? How much of your self-respect would you sacrifice for a weak compromise? How do you decide how far to go when every challenge has a new set of rules?"

You don't have to do anything you don't want to. You only have to justify yourself to your opinion. Your instincts energize your self-respect. Maybe you need a push. Maybe you need a dozen pushes. You're not a slave to time. You're not a slave to anyone's opinion. A friend's encouragement should be supportive, not a challenge you're not ready for. We all need help in making commitments. It takes confidence. It's the belief in yourself that honors your self-respect so your patience will trust it.

You do your best but maybe you didn't make the team or you were passed over for that promotion. You thought you were good. You thought you did well. But you became part of someone else's self-respect. You entered their sphere of challenges. It was their decision whether or not to include you. You still think you deserve it. The solution to what you want isn't in your circumstances. It's in *You*. A "failure" identifies, for whatever reason, that situation wasn't in your best interests. Someone else got the job. Someone else got to play. They wanted it just as much as you did. God's energy competes with itself to form alliances. So part of your job is learning to trust your frustrations. You'll never force a solution past God's plan. You're part of a bigger picture. There's always another door open for you. See what works. Feel your disappointment then get back to business. Don't waste your time crying. Self-pity is a bandage not an answer.

Unsolvable is your insistence on something that's not right for you. It might be right later but not for now. It may never be. Accepting it is an accomplishment. There's a benefit to everything. Focus on the opportunities you know. Weigh the values. The seed of an accomplishment wants to do better. You may have to change your plan. It's not that you made a mistake. You made a decision. You considered the alternatives and picked what you thought was best. It takes courage. You have to trust yourself. It's your self-respect talking to you.

Without self-respect all that's left are social ideals; currently at the maturity level of a young teenager. You're always yourself but you want to fit in. Human beings are social animals. It could be Saturday night at a dance club or volunteering for a community project. You want to enjoy yourself and support your neighbors. You share similar experiences so you have similar values. You want Peace with your neighbors. You want to feel good about yourself. But instead of mutual respect, groupthink can force you to match immature values. Then self-respect depends on your spiritual instinct. It takes courage to love society when so many people don't care. You still have to support yourself. Sincerity means you can change your mind when you find a better way. Marching in step with a group is great as long as that group respects you.

You can punish yourself. You can lose patience and get angry with yourself. You want to succeed so much that you make unrealistic demands on yourself. You stop loving yourself. In your effort to support your self-respect you sacrifice it. Self-punishment is a trap. It makes you the victim of your own impatience. Respect your faith. Trust Love. Protect your self-respect. You literally have all the time in the world. There's no need to hurt yourself. Self-punishment is a simplistic response to life's confusion. You're better than that. You can find a solution that includes Love. In your heart you know it. Trust yourself. You may think you first have to settle past wrongs. Do what you can then move on. Keep your thoughts on Love. You'll fix things when the right time comes. Don't sacrifice your opportunities by hurting yourself. It's not for you to judge. Find Peace in your sincerity. Stay above the fray and respect yourself.

The other side of confusion is narcissism. It defines self-respect as a fantasy, an imaginary belief of what success is. The success may be real but narcissism makes its importance greater than its value. Its purpose is self-importance. It's personal so it's different for everyone. But it's a sweet game gone sour. You wrongly see yourself as deficient so you think your self-respect depends on having an inflated opinion of yourself. Self-respect only depends on what you want it to be. Your life is God's expression. You're as important as anything else in Creation. Self-respect is your appreciation of the free will God gave you. Your only limit is God's plan. No one else's opinion is needed.

You can create any solution you want. You won't be happy with everything God planned for you. You have your own ideas. You have your own plans. You may think God is too limited. You may think it takes too long. Self-respect demands the right solution even when it's not what you want. Intuitively you know you'll be okay. You can survive anything. You just have to find harmony with it. You have a partner in God. You can feel it. Now you have to work with it. The results prove themselves as each piece falls into place and you know you made the right decision. It's encouraging. Nurture that courage. In time, you'll see the limitless benefits you create together. It's comforting to know you have a partner who can bend Creation into whatever it wants.

Accept the timing. If you want an instant solution you're better off praying. Only God can do that. It might happen but it's not necessary. You'll feel relieved but it's more important to get it right. It's important to learn the lesson. You don't want to waste the opportunity your soul waited for. You don't want to spend more than you have to, and you don't want to be so cheap the problem doesn't get solved. The curious thing is how God's solution comes before you even ask. The path is planned. That's how it starts. You enter life's maze. It takes as long as it has to. You want to learn something or why bother? Your image of Peace is less important than learning to be confident with your doubts.

Look at the achievements in medicine and you can see when those suffering can now regain their health. Advances in stem cell therapies, robotics, and artificial intelligence highlight opportunities for anyone who thought their predicament was hopeless. Things progress because it's human nature to improve ourselves. We share the challenge of survival. One person's observation becomes another's education to create the skills that become someone else's invention. New ideas are refined through universal consciousness and everyone benefits. We share this mystery of consciousness. It connects us. Human experience is God's way to question its existence as we meet the mystery together in God's Love.

Nature provides endless choices so appreciate the differences. They're all opportunities. Every person has a purpose and the resources to accomplish it even if it means first failing. Since our purposes are aligned we should help each other. There are compromises to make and opportunities to share. Self-respect is your mandate to fulfill your dream. It controls the balance between your resources and responsibilities. You're born and you hit the ground running. You don't need a better way. Self-respect works perfectly. It's your job even if the best you get out of it is an education. It's important because your education educates God. Or you can coast through life like a nondescript piece of furniture. But why give up before you even try? Your future is now. You can still win.

Self-respect is in your mind, so it's your decision how to use it. Life is all around you but you don't need life to inspire you. You're born with self-importance. It's God's way to help you see your place in Creation. It's your soul. It's your connection to God's universal soul. No authority, no boss or government, can take it from you. They can take your money and your freedom, but no one can take your self-respect. It's in your heart. It's in your beliefs about yourself. You can reveal it however you like. You might be tricked into giving it away but you can take it back whenever you want. Your self-respect is your respect for God. When you regret something, it's your self-respect that accepts it. Self-respect forgives your disappointments. But it's emotional so it can take time to know it.

You have to own your self-respect. You decide its limits. The world expects you to know that, and if you don't it's your tough luck. Most people won't show you how. They're dealing with their own self-respect. Or they may feel it's an intrusion; it's your responsibility and they don't want to impose on your desperation. Like the old W.C. Fields line, "Never give a sucker an even break and never wisen up a chump." It's up to you to make yourself wise. It's common sense to trust yourself. You create problems when you doubt yourself. You wind up believing you're incapable of making a good decision. It's a lack of confidence. No one knows everything. We all have to learn. Others got through it and you will too. Wisdom is your belief that your self-respect guides you. Self-respect is Nature's gyroscope. It knows you're important so it keeps you on track.

Who should you ask for advice? Who do you trust? Most people don't know much more than you do. Even with the same problems their perspective is colored by their own values. But it might be the best advice you can get. Don't be satisfied because it's easy and don't reject it because it's easy. Be sincere and you'll find what you need. Go online. Read a book. Talk about your problem with friends. Someone will help you. Everyone needs advice. Most people like giving advice. It reinforces a positive opinion of themselves. Advice can come from anywhere. How to make money? How to be healthy? How to find love? How to be happy? People want to improve their lives. More than a specific result, self-respect wants you to be confident in your ability. Self-respect wants you to be your own trusted advisor.

Your self-respect wants you to succeed. That's its ambition. That's why it tests you. It wants you to trust Love and trust your common sense. There's always a conflict between your visionary side, your free will, and your practical side, what it takes to make it happen. Life is a risk. You might suffer if you fail and nobody wants to suffer. "What career should you choose? Who should you marry?" How can you make a fair compromise when it's all so confusing? Who makes the rules? People have different opinions. Some you'll agree with and some you won't. Ask yourself, "What are their values? What are their arguments? What are their priorities?" You may not have the experience so you rely on your self-respect. Your self-respect wants what's right for you and, through God's wisdom; it wants what's right for everyone. And if you make a mistake, trust your sincerity will fix it.

Those are the problems. The results can be whatever you want. But you won't be happy if you don't respect yourself. Without self-respect you'll always be less than who you could have been. It's important to remember there can be different right answers. Going through a stop sign is okay when a person needs immediate help. It's a question of values. Life is choices. That's how it works. That's its purpose, to question your choices. That's why we have courts to decide what's fair. It's how a society keeps its balance when circumstances force someone past their limits. It has rules for mutual respect. Nothing is unsolvable. Unsolvable means a lack of imagination. Sometimes you have to adapt to a bigger picture. Sometimes it's best to move on. Dogma takes the least effort because you don't have to think about it. But it's static. It doesn't grow. A good solution proves itself by evolving with its environment. That's why life exists; to create opportunities where Love can explore new environments.

Your self-respect questions your values. Do you have to be first in everything you do? When should you consider others? What's fair considering the situation? Are you valuing everything correctly? How should you negotiate when you only have to answer to yourself? Should you leave a note on that parked car you backed into? Do you take pride in your honesty or would you rather enjoy the convenience in a lie? Justice is the social equivalent of self-respect. You stand by your mistakes in the same way you stand up for your opinion, not because you have to but because it's the right thing to do. It trusts the implicit fairness in Creation. When you respect fairness, you trust God will be fair to you too. It has to. It's all one thing.

Chapter 1
Your Personal Environment

"Think outside the box." You've heard that a thousand times. Don't limit yourself. Trust yourself. Explore your opportunities. Life reveals itself in the unexpected detours. That's how it teaches you lessons you weren't even aware of. If you can't find a better way, then make one. Poke at it. See what happens. Ask what you can do with it. But that's only half the story. Reality is two boxes. There's the box of your imagination and what you can create. And there's the box of the life you lead every day that you can arrange any way you like. They're both barriers and opportunities. It's life's limits and your soul's vision of what you can do with it.

That's everything. Once you negotiate those boxes you can do anything. First, life presents barriers in the confusion of inexperience. It demands that you learn how to do things. The process began in your mother's womb. As you explored your awareness you twisted and turned till you found a safe place to grow. Then you're born into consciousness and your talent for questioning blossoms. Your creative soul joined your human intellect to become the living expression of God's opportunities. You discovered you had abilities. So you practiced stacking blocks. You saw how high you could go without tipping them over. Then you added toys. You moved them around till you were satisfied how they balanced. You added rules and created games. Everything your creativity would use for the rest of your life started there.

It's the same way God makes the rules you live by. You get tired so you have to rest. If you don't, your body doesn't work and you can't think straight. You rest and you're good again. Positive thinking is important but some things will never happen no matter what you believe. You'll never be as small as an ant or as big as a skyscraper. Your ability to be those things doesn't exist. You can always lay on your belly for an ant's point of view or take the elevator to the roof. You express your goals through what you *can* do. You approach every question logically but you need your creativity to take Nature's impossibilities and work them into solutions you can trust. You often have to wait till life catches up and creates them. Or you have to wait till the wind dies down.

It's a game but God won't toy with you. Well, maybe a little. God has a sense of humor too. Remember your wry smile when someone says, "Someday we'll look back on this and laugh." Life is God's game. It's joyful, brutal, generous, and demanding. Like all games, it has a beginning and an end. The point is in life's game winning and losing make no difference. It's like playing catch. It's just a game. Enjoy it. Everyone throws their experience into the pot so God can learn more about itself. Love's experience is life's meaning and you win just by being here even if you keep your eyes closed.

Like the weather, some rules affect everyone. You may have a fifty dollar umbrella but everyone wants to stay dry even if it means wearing a shopping bag on their head. Other rules affect just you, like spraining your back when you overdo an exercise. Some have a family history of heart disease and others share a genetic disposition for perfect teeth. These differences frame your environment. Your environment is the stage for your experience. It's not your physical environment, like the difference between living in the country and living in the city. It's the environment of your personality configured through your experience. It's your gender, race, nationality, age, religion, appearance, sexuality, occupation, reputation, talents, predilections, intelligence, education, aptitudes, attitudes, values, priorities, resources, interests, health, finances, family, community, integrity, and all the cultural groups you belong to. It covers everything life means to you. It's your burdens and opportunities. It's how you spend your time. It's your thoughts about everything. It's your beliefs and the starting point for your goals. It's your character. In this incredible stew, we're all the same. We all love success and hate disappointment.

You choose the rules you live by. They're easy to see when you're honest with yourself. It could be your diet or the respect you expect from others. It's definable. Whatever you include must follow those rules. It's the pattern you create for yourself. Your choices accommodate the pattern so you can be comfortable with them. Outside the rules is unfamiliar and uncomfortable.

SELF-RESPECT: THE SOLUTION TO UNSOLVABLE PROBLEMS

It's uncertain. So you ask yourself, "Is it safe? Can you trust it? Should you fear it? How can you work with it?" It's like a stranger you meet in the street. You want to get along but you're not sure how. There's fear on both sides. The characters are unfamiliar and the game board looks odd. What should you expect? There are different demands, but are there really?

Life is the same everywhere. People survive. It's all one mind. Everyone wants good things for themselves and they want to avoid the bad things. It makes sense. But dependable traditions can run their course. An increase in population requires more to support them. New ideas are needed. It tests a community's creativity. Outside the box is a new frame of reference. It has its own rules. It already exists but you can change it. You can make adjustments. You can change the environment or change your attitude about it. The laws of physics are the same. It's like learning a foreign language. Whatever you communicate still must serve your self-respect. You just have to learn the rules. You have to learn the customs. It feels odd at first, but it's always your home because it's designed with self-respect in mind.

Accommodating new rules can feel strange. A serious illness or sudden wealth has unique demands. And your daily decisions depend on those demands before you even address the mundane parts of life. How will you eat when you can't feed yourself? How will you protect your money when someone lies to you? Inside the box are trusted alliances, family and friends, even the convenience store clerk where you buy your coffee every morning. It's easy to negotiate with people you know. You trust your experience. At least you're familiar with it. But it's not enough. When you create a new box, old relationships may not like your new values. You become a stranger. Your new values become an unknown and many people have enough trouble negotiating with people they know. The question is, "Will a new box make you happier?"

Everything has limits. "Inside the box" has limits you know. But "outside the box" has unknown limits. Instead, it sees endless opportunities for innovation. Everyone has the same problems. "How do you survive? How do you improve yourself?" That's the difference between you and Nature. With God's creativity you can engineer new solutions. A bird can drop a rock on a clam and break it open, but human beings, besides smashing the clam, can promote the whole process. They mine the ore, make the steel, design the product, build a device to form it, make it, sell it, buy it, shuck some clams, and then create a festival for it. And they make improvements along the way. The connections are infinite because you can create whatever you like. Like God, you can arrange Creation to fit your vision. You question the Universe and share the answers with God. That's the deal.

A bird's consciousness is confined to the limits of its nature. Your consciousness as an extension of God is unlimited because, like God, whatever you imagine you can create. That's the beauty in atomic structure. It's the same as the building blocks in your playpen. You put them together to make what you wanted and filled in the spaces with your imagination. Like professional sports, you take the simple concept of moving a ball on a field and make it so complex you need a playbook three inches thick to remember what you're doing.

Free will adds your consciousness to the universal experience. Your effort affects everyone. Everything gets repurposed through your perspective. Love is the ultimate perspective. To succeed, it must be shared. A reasonable person can't see another person suffering and not want to help them. It's Love's nature. It's your window on consciousness. It has no limit. It doesn't take much effort. It takes more effort to resist it. Love can be frightening. It reveals your vulnerabilities. You're used to protecting yourself. Everyone isn't open-minded. They may have shut down their feelings a long time ago. For them, it's dog eat dog. This is your environment. You do your best to feed yourself while your soul keeps asking…right or wrong, fair or not? You want to love everyone but you have to love yourself too.

You always answer to Nature. Life forces it on you. You need to breathe. You need sustenance. You need health, hope, and freedom. It's inescapable. When you're denied any of those you suffer. Your needs compel you. Your self-respect demands it. It's your comfort and satisfaction. You're responsible for taking care of yourself. Self-respect is your reality. There's no escape. There's no need to escape. This is what it is to be human. This is what you signed up for. These are the rules your soul must follow. These are the rules your creativity respects. Life says, "Do better." Then your self-respect aligns you with God's purpose.

With society come businesses, schools, hospitals, religious centers, charities, museums, parks, garbage pick-up, public works projects, and emergency

SELF-RESPECT: THE SOLUTION TO UNSOLVABLE PROBLEMS

services. These are the answers to society's needs. Self-respect is the answer to your needs. It's the box that defines you. Is a new pair of shoes more important or are music lessons your priority? What's more immediate? What's best for later? What doesn't matter at all? Everyone's needs are personal. Maybe you like spring water and you're repulsed by that alcoholic drink with the little umbrella in it. Or maybe you like the complex flavors in a casserole and to you an apple is just plain food. Every choice is a responsibility because you decide when your hunger is satisfied. You decide what's important to you at the moment.

Then where do you draw the line that respects everyone? What defines it? How do you include someone who doesn't want to be included? The answers reveal how a society respects itself. It has to include all the boxes we use to define ourselves. It has to include the reaction we expect. The question is, "Are you satisfied with the fairness in your actions?" Does it make good sense to help each other, or "Abandon ship! Everyone for themselves!" But maybe you're not really sinking. Maybe it just means compromising. Self-respect is a value judgment. You're responsible for defending your limits. But once you're satisfied then what? You're in good health. You have a home. You have goals. You have resources. But what does your self-respect ask when you see someone suffering? Without good sanitation your problem isn't which craft beer to drink. It's how not to get sick.

It's a big world and you have your own problems. But the media doesn't think you're as interesting as a feud between two celebrities you never heard of. The truth is the media, your source for the information that keeps you safe, is lazy. It prefers dramatic images to useful answers. It's entertainment. It likes fires and fighting; anything to inflame your emotions while you stay safe at home. Human beings have different values but they're basically reasonable. The quiet misery of overdose deaths is ignored. It's rarely as exciting as an old hurricane on TV. It's fun watching someone's roof blow off. Wow. And when an honest person explains it, there's always a naysayer to say, "No." It's all human nature. I'd like to see a show that keeps the guests coming back to the same question and makes them continually prove the facts with new evidence that can be checked and refuted at subsequent shows; a public trial with the truth as the defendant. You may not like the judgment but it's not about winning. It's about trusting the facts. What you do with them is your business.

People want a safe direction but the media doesn't like good news. It takes work to make it interesting. Danger focuses your attention. It's a threat that must be dealt with. Achievement takes determination; a boring kind of enthusiasm that takes a long time and a lot of work. The media wants tragedy now with trilling sirens and horrible screams. It's easy money. There's no respect for the audience, just manipulating an absorbed public to buy more products. So we get incessant coverage of missing airplanes with nothing to see. Then who'll solve the mystery? "What's the difference?" Problems come with hardships. They burden the human soul. Watching people starve isn't exciting. It makes you want to turn away. Watching people attack a relief truck is exciting. Hungry people need food. They need hope. You either work to do better or live with the chaos. Your soul knows the difference. That's its beauty. One good thought can make everything right.

Once a threat passes all you want is a comfortable place to be yourself. Life is a pleasure again. You can put a new picture on the wall. You can work ten hours a day. Whatever satisfies you. Comfort is your proof. Comfort is feeling safe. Your thoughts are free to do what every human being does when they have everything...whatever you like. You can enjoy your aspirations. That or get drunk because you can't turn yourself off. You're always thinking about something. You can act in a play or hide in a cave. You can imagine anything and do it. Or, like most, you can ask God to help you answer the question, "What am I here for?"

Life's mystery is God's gift and you touch it with every thought. You can arrange it however you like and see what it does. Have a positive attitude and it could surprise you. Question yourself, "Can you make things better by changing something?" By refining your questions to a single thought you can cover every combination possible. Just ask, "Good or bad?" then you're free to make it whatever you like. From God's imagination it becomes your imagination. So "problems" are simply a matter of turning undesirable combinations into favorable ones, i.e. "solutions." If you want something different, change it. Respect your ability. Respect your purpose. It doesn't matter what it takes. It only matters that you do it. Waiting for it to happen on its own could take beyond your lifetime.

SELF-RESPECT: THE SOLUTION TO UNSOLVABLE PROBLEMS

Self-respect is life's balance. It's how you manage it. Life expresses Love's consciousness. It's your physical, emotional, intellectual, and spiritual being. It's the sum of your psychic awareness. Consciousness is the difference between joy, suffering, and a tolerant attitude. It sets the stage where your values perform. It tells you when you have everything and when there's something missing.

Your soul accepts you for who you are. It loves you the way you are. It helps you promote a conscious connection between you and God. You have responsibilities to God as well as to the life you chose. Your soul has responsibilities to the challenge God planned for you. Fulfilling your responsibilities can be complex, but no more complicated than helping a friend read a map. It shares responsibilities to help deal with the problem. You ask for help when you need it and you do what you can when you're needed.

That's what's meant by, "Life mimics heaven." The principles of existence are the same. Physics is the same. Logic is the same. Love is the same. Every situation makes sense when compared to a similar situation. You have the ability to understand any concept. Maybe it's explained in a word or maybe it takes a college library. In truth, you're better. Through your soul you're hard-wired into the Universe. It's common for people in the same field to change definitions so unless you're an insider it sounds like a foreign language, whether it's hip slang or industry jargon. People like to identify with the uniqueness of being "in the know." Clarity is the ability to identify a concept with a meaning understandable to anyone. That's communication. That's respect. It's all the parts of the Universe working together.

Your self-respect wants you to improve. It's instinctive. You build on experience so it takes your whole life. Your self-respect wants you to succeed whether it's trying a new haircut or changing careers. To improve means you're always in uncharted territories pushing beyond the limits you know. But no matter where you are in the psychic boxes you live, you'll need courage. Your environment is limited by the life you choose. It's like someone with a handicap who refuses to let it stop them from competition. They won't accept the limits of their disability even if it's justifiable. They want what they want and they accept they'll just have to do what it takes. They accept less because it's the best they can do. They just want to be sure they've tried everything because they still want what they *can* have.

There are always limits. Limits are life's requirements, like baseball where you're not allowed to run outside the base paths. Knowing your employer is the best path to getting a job. It's not fair but it's legitimate. You help the people you know. You hire family members because you love each other. It doesn't matter if it limits you to their skill level. It's sharing Love and you can always teach them what to do. Limits are exclusive. You have to be strong enough to lift the weight. You have to be smart enough to know what's best. You have to care. It's never an individual's background. Life is economic. It's about survival. It's about competition. The reliable moneymaker is always first in line regardless of where they came from. Prejudice is just an easy way of saying, "Me first!"

"Me first!" has its place. Your first responsibility is to yourself. Plus you're responsible to those who share your background. Everyone needs support from someone who understands them. They appreciate you because they know your limits. You go out of your way for them and they go out of their way for you. They teach you and you teach them. It's how the game works. Life isn't all problems. It's solutions. I saw a TV documentary about a Jewish neighborhood. They went to a kosher butcher and asked if they could film there. They told the butcher he would be on television. The butcher said he didn't care because he didn't own a television, but "anything to help a Jew make a living." We love each other, but everyone has to survive. That's the tricky part. That's where Love helps. It smooths out the differences. Then you have to decide. Those pesky values again. Frozen whale blubber may not be to your liking, but everyone has to eat and you eat what you can get.

Tools make a difference. They amplify your abilities. They make problem-solving easier. Tools give you control you wouldn't have without them. They inspire you to do more. They make you super-human whether it's a hammer or an MRI scanner. Have you ever tried to put a screw in with your fingers? It doesn't work. You need a screwdriver to make it tight. It could be a stepstool to help you reach a light bulb you want to change. Without it, it's impossible. Knowledge is a tool. Ask anyone who's trained for a career. And a career is a great tool for paying the bills. It could be a chart to compare things or an alliance to multiply your strength. Tools extend your vision as you find

SELF-RESPECT: THE SOLUTION TO UNSOLVABLE PROBLEMS

new ways to use them. Your most important tool is your determination. It's your soul demanding success. You can change anything. You just need the right tool. Nature is a superbly designed tool to create opportunities. Respect it. It's a lot bigger than you, but it answers to your self-respect.

Life takes work. You have to push hard to make the status quo make room for you. But you don't have to wait a million years for the rain to wear away the rocks. You can change it today with an air hammer. Your creativity is the greatest tool you have. Your nature is to make your environment work for you. Your strength is you can do whatever you like. So do it. It's the foundation for your self-respect. Educate yourself. Expand your awareness. Education doesn't mean sacrificing yourself to someone else's point of view. Education is your opportunity to question life through the accomplishments of others. Your experience contributes to the universal context that creates opportunities for everyone. It's the perfect foundation for your questions. That's what God wants. Your perspective is critical. So what's on your mind? Your feelings are more ethereal. You sense them but they're hard to define. You're describing spiritual energy. You're touching your soul's vibration. You're touching God. It's the sixth sense of an expert hunter who always knows where the game is. It's your free will. It's beyond human nature. Your feelings excite your intentions and your intentions excite your thoughts. They beckon you to share God's consciousness. Like a prayer, you're asking God for help. When you acknowledge God it's easier to trust yourself. It justifies your self-respect. Now you know you'll find the right balance. Now you have Love's source to guide you. Intelligence is limited because it depends on repeating expectations. God will show you anything is possible when you use your imagination. It's where miracles happen despite your expectations. Then life can show you what it is, not what you think you control. Civilization calls it an invention. But the physics were always there. You added the vision. You gave it a purpose. You have the ability to see things in new ways. That's always your intention; to find a new way.

Changing your environment isn't as easy as just shuffling the deck. A card game is a simple puzzle. It doesn't take long to play. It has a beginning and an end. But life is endless puzzles jumbled together with the pieces close enough to fit even when the pictures aren't the same. That's the difference. That's where your creativity shines. You can make new rules. You can change the connections. You can re-create the environment. Your environment is your life and your life is a mixture of all your puzzles. It's your ability to expand Nature by combining things in new ways. Like any game, a problem leads you to a sequence of choices. It's the difference between the dependability of your desk phone and the mobility of your cell phone. You choose what's more important. Self-respect asks you to question what's best at the moment. Your soul's intent makes you the leader. But in a Universe of free-thinking individuals there are many leaders…and endless puzzles.

Survival is your responsibility. You have to take care of yourself. You have to get along with others. We depend on each other so you have to nurture your relationships. You have to deal with everyone's moods; from your spouse to the clerk on the phone. You get a sense of who you like, who you trust, and how much you trust them. It's manageable. It's a mature attitude. But maturity takes time. That's why you shouldn't lose hope. You have to trust Love's timing. You can stress out about it but wisdom tells you to be patient. Maturity is small steps over time. Then you amaze yourself with what you can do, like speaking in front of a crowd. Life is challenges, successes, setbacks, and then you go again. That's how it is. That's how you live with it. You don't have to like it but you have to find Peace with it. Life is familiar. You can resent it if you don't mind being miserable or accept it and do your best. Be proud of yourself for trying. Hope may be the only way left, but it's a sensible one.

Society asks you to have good relationships even when you'd rather be alone. It's important to respect society. It's not important to be the most popular. It helps if you're competing in business. Society's approval is how you make your living. But as far as your opinion of yourself, you have a place that must be respected. Don't expect others to care about you. Don't expect others to pity you. Everyone has their own needs. They have themselves to consider. You're always responsible for yourself, especially in your compromises. Whatever help you get is a welcome extra. Respect your values and respect Love. It's the right thing to do. Take pride in your reputation. It's the image of self-respect you project to society. It's the measure of trust you can expect in return.

You might think you can't do it so you make an excuse. You might even believe your excuse. But it's not real no matter how much comfort it gives

SELF-RESPECT: THE SOLUTION TO UNSOLVABLE PROBLEMS

you. It's a lazy escape, a justification, and an illusion. It means you can stop working because what you want is impossible. But maybe it's doable tomorrow. Maybe you'll dream of a way overnight. A new invention may be the headline of tomorrow's news...and it'll solve your problem. Your happiness is always possible. That's a good mantra for your self-respect. *There's always a way.* You just have to see it from the right angle. If you have a problem ask yourself, "What could change things in your favor?"

Maybe you don't have the experience. Maybe you're too young and everything's new to you. Maybe it's a new technology. It's not the end of the world. You need patience when you try something new. You need time to gather your thoughts. You need time to learn how to do it. And you need help whether it's learning arithmetic or the new software at work. It's the wisdom of self-respect. It doesn't diminish you if you don't know how. Everyone needs help; helpless babies, clueless teenagers, confused college kids, overworked parents, desperate job-seekers, and aimless retirees. You go as far as you can then you get help. And when the next hapless soul comes along, you pay it back by helping them. When you share your self-respect, Creation smiles.

Self-respect is your psychic environment. You can be honest, make it up, or ignore it altogether. Then what should you believe in? Is it the media hullabaloo? Is it the face of suffering? Is it a celebrity's testimonial? Is it fabulous wealth? Or is it a story of hope, because if you don't get relief you're going to jump off a bridge. You can't ignore it. Your sympathy won't let you. This is where your self-respect lives. It's the burden of human nature balanced by your soul's purpose. It's Love at work. It's never perfect so you have to deal with it. It may be perfect in God's eyes, but for you it's a pain in the neck. And there's nowhere to hide. So how do you live with it? You can make the music louder. You can bring more beauty to life. You can take a walk, find a hobby, or read a book. Build your life where you are. Don't stop working on it. The target of your creativity is your self-respect. You define it. It's what God meant for you. It's the solution to everything.

In the grand scheme of things, your problems don't matter. It's a trick life plays on you. Problems are the way God questions your values. Your happiness is in the balance, but there's little you can do about it. Just hope for the best and be logical. See what happens. While you wait you might as well feel good about yourself. At least, be fair to yourself. You can't guarantee you won't get sick or be late for a meeting. But you don't have to identify with it. You don't have to let the possibility of having a problem define you. Then how do you know how you're doing? Are you better than that person across the street even though you know very little about them? Are your pleasures worthwhile or merely the conquests your culture admires? What's your self-respect missing if you need someone to tell you what it should be? Who are you trying to impress? Is it someone who would step over you if they saw you lying in the street or someone who would sacrifice their life to see you went to college? If you want to respect yourself you have to know these things.

Material achievements can substitute for self-respect. They measure life tangibly, win or lose, so they're easy to understand. It's another day's survival. You cheer for yourself because you won the moment. The cost doesn't matter. You do it because it creates the life you want. But life has consequences beyond the daily standings. It's more than win or lose. Did you get that job and now you can move to a bigger house? Did you get an approving look from your future spouse with the hope of having a family? Did you get the sale price on the furniture so now you can buy more holiday gifts? With life you want to win every time. You don't care about justifying a loss. Ask yourself if you measure your life in comparison to others or are you happy with what you want? Do you own your self-respect? By that measure you're always successful because winning is believing in yourself. There's no one else to convince. Just you.

You love watching a blowout, a sports event where your hero annihilates the competition. It takes the tension out of the game and you can enjoy the victory without the stress of a fight. You want your life to be as easy as possible. You just want to win, like everyone else. Then there's the satisfaction in watching two equally matched boxers beat the hell out of each other till the final round. They trained for this moment and they both want to win. They understand hard work and sacrifice. Taking blows and giving blows, standing up and never giving up. Then, exhausted and bleeding, they collapse on each other at the final bell; thrilled at surviving, respecting themselves for the fight they gave, and respecting their opponent. You admire that. You respect it. No matter what the judges' score, you see them both as winners

SELF-RESPECT: THE SOLUTION TO UNSOLVABLE PROBLEMS

and so do they. It's the character of self-respect that they did their best. That's as much as anyone can do.

It's the same for you. You fight every day in the most competitive arena there is, life. It's not your battle with other commuters. It's your battle with yourself in your fight for self-respect. Life's a challenge. You may have to struggle for a seat on the bus and then question yourself if you should give it up to a child. A pregnant woman with too many packages is an easy choice. But life isn't about easy choices. It's a struggle for peace of mind in the values of the moment. It's where you ask endless questions because you can't turn them off. It tests your sincerity under pressure. It's a continuous stress test. Like those two boxers, congratulate yourself for the battles you fought not just your victories. Know you did your best. Your challenge is to live a full life with what you have and never give up.

There's a pot of gold at the end of the rainbow. It's your self-respect when you achieve your ambition. You want something. It could be a breath of fresh air or a college degree, but you want it. God's blessing is that you define it. It's your right to compare the Peace in your self-respect to how it could be better. Should you keep what you have or risk it on something else? "I'll take door number three, Monte." like the TV game show asked the contestants to risk what they already won. Achievements are important. But there are new worlds to conquer, even if it means a role in the retirement home follies. There's no age limit for your imagination. "I needed that!" you say as you fill your lungs with the salty, sea air or "I've done it!" as they hand you your diploma. These are spiritual achievements. They include the Love you leaned on in your doubts. They say more than you won the battle. They shout you won the war.

Self-respect is stronger than fear because it trusts your confidence. It supports your awareness of God's role in everything. Everything's connected. It's not about a victory where the victor gets the spoils. Success means everyone wins. It's the solution that satisfies everyone. Self-respect asks you to be fair. Selfishness may seem like a quick way to success, but it's limited by self-aggrandizement. It's limited by thinking you're bigger than the Universe. While patting yourself on the back, you turn away from everything the Universe can do for you. Creation doesn't grow with one winner. It would get stuck, limited by such a narrow path. Self-respect is the inspiration of spiritual victories built on each other. They support each other. It's the success of everything you admire. It isn't bought or sold. It's cherished and shared.

This is your environment. It's the complicated world of other people's opinions in the same way you take your turn at a four-way stop sign. Whose turn is it now? It's the uncertain world of negotiating your self-respect with everyone you meet. You want a fair deal but you'd love a great deal. You just don't want a deal you'll regret. Everything is an agreement between you and Nature. It's not the nature of meadows and trees, but it's just as natural. It's the nature of Love and survival, two things you do well. The challenge is how to accommodate the creativity of your human nature with the wildness of Earth's nature. Add technology and it can change pretty fast.

Humanity's survival is the growth of ideas. Ideas are the spiritual side of human nature. Ideas ask for God's help because you always want something more. Ambition drives your self-respect. You want more action or you want more peace. It could be a bigger house or better food. It could be playing sports in the park or lingering at the museum. Whatever you think is good for you, you want. From choosing what to wear to texting a friend, you want it to be your best. Love is always your best. Your soul supports Love in everything you do. It starts with your self-respect. It may sound odd you would want anything that's not good for you but that's the funny part. You only have one direction; to do what you think would be better.

Your body is another story. It's autonomous. It takes care of itself without much attention. If you stub your toe, it'll heal and return you to a healthy balance. It has natural defenses as your toe forms a callous to protect it. But you can help it. You can buy more comfortable shoes. You can medicate yourself for the pain or wear a brace for support. You can exercise to build strength in your toe. With your desire to do more, you can improve your toe's health. Nature by itself can't do it exactly the way you want. It'll keep you healthy but in its own way. You have to guide it if you want it to be what you want. You don't want the unexpected consequence of your toe healing improperly. It may not perform the way you want. You have to lead your body. With your attention you can make it better than it could ever be without you.

SELF-RESPECT: THE SOLUTION TO UNSOLVABLE PROBLEMS

Your body values its health. If you overexert yourself it'll slow you down. You're exhausted. You get tired. It says, "Rest now. Nothing is more important." You can will yourself to go on but not more than you're physically able. Your body has limits. But you decide your values. Is it worth putting in a 60 hour work week at the chance of weakening your immune system and getting sick? It's your mental health too. A healthy mind supports your self-respect. You know not to make an important decision when you're tired. Your mind is too distracted to consider all the possibilities. A healthy mind has no limits. The healthier it is, the more you trust it. Everything evolves. What started out as a game in the street became billion dollar sports teams playing in multi-million dollar arenas for millions of people. Life develops in its own way. It doesn't have to be what you intended. Your creation becomes the nourishment future generations build on. Your soul connects you to everything. Love is your soul's health. You can share it everywhere because its only limit is Creation. And with Creation you can do anything.

It's likely you call your limits *problems*. So by accepting that limit you eliminate the problem. It becomes an issue, something of no consequence to be solved or forgotten. Problems are often about timing, being late for the train or taking too long to grow up. Time organizes activity but it's not a problem unless you make it a problem. It's a consideration. The beauty is you have the ability to change time. You can create alternatives to any schedule. You can leave ten minutes early and not have to rush for the train. You can have more experiences so you mature faster. You can eliminate a task and give yourself time for other things. It recognizes the spiritual core of a problem because delays can work in your favor. Your doctor's appointment might be canceled so now you have time to see a friend. But you never know the future, so use common sense and respect your time.

Logic says, "Trust what you know." Logic's odd wrinkle is defenselessness supports your trust. It doesn't mean you don't protect yourself. It means you don't worry about it. You trust God so there's no need to fear your defenses could fail. There's no need to fear even when common sense challenges you. Miracles happen all the time. It's easy to say when fear is such a big part of your protection, but you know how fear limits you. You hold back or jump too soon. Trust God's plan. Believe you'll do well. That should be your identity: "Somehow you'll find a way to win." Expect it. You can still buy that lottery ticket but have the good sense to work hard at your job. You'll see it all works together. Things evolve. They develop into new things. Don't suffer life's limits. Life is what you imagine...so imagine good things.

Your environment is an important part of the game. It's the background for your questions. It challenges you by hiding the answers right in front of you. Finding the answers is the way you win. It's a weird mystery when success means you have to overcome a hardship. If you lived just one life, good or bad, so what? You die and it's over. It would be easy. You'd just disappear. But your consciousness is never over. You're an eternal being, an eternal consciousness, with a purpose beyond your survival. You may think wealth is your success. You may think the suffering you survived is an achievement. You may think it's important that people like you. People will do what they believe is in their best interests. Those who love you will enjoy your success. Strangers will envy you and see you as a ripe plum to pick. People are impressed with the victory they wish was theirs. In your eternal consciousness the important thing success means is to have hope. Winning the lottery feels great but it's one in ten million. Hope you can have every day just by wanting it.

If owning things defines your self-respect then good fortune defines your happiness. But why not be happy all the time? Grab your happiness when you can, good times or bad, even if it's just a good laugh. You'll feel better. What you can't change is no reason to suffer it. And what does it say about life when you die? Did you satisfy your eternal being? If not, what more could you have done? Creation is your unlimited wealth. Free will is your self-respect. Money imitates wealth because it makes things happen. Self-respect means, money or not, you make things happen.

Things don't define self-respect. Self-respect is an attitude. It's what you believe about yourself. You can make something important or ignore it. You can even risk your life for it. Ask an adventurer...or any mother. If you can afford it, it's fun to have nice things. You should enjoy what you can afford. The economics of buying things helps everyone; from the lumberjack who cuts the trees that build your house to the real estate agent who sells it. But if you can't afford it, you have to know your self-respect is intact. Self-respect is in your mind. It's in your soul. Your soul demands Love. But once you have it,

SELF-RESPECT: THE SOLUTION TO UNSOLVABLE PROBLEMS

life's an endless exploration of its wonders and a never-ending quest to create more Love.

You don't live just one life. You live many lives as your soul tests each incarnation in a new environment, both physical and emotional. We ceremoniously bury our loved ones. We sadden at the sight of an unmarked grave and those who loved them left to guess what happened. Love connects us beyond death. Love is eternal. Multiple lives work perfectly with Eternity. Why else would you sense a responsibility for your behavior once you're dead? Without Love, the deceased would be no more than scrap to be cast out with the trash. No sane person would accept that. Love is an unbreakable bond. So if Eternity is real and opportunities never end then multiple lives is the perfect way for Creation to grow. Self-respect becomes an eternal concept and life's problems exercise for the soul. The result of exercise is strength. Life creates the tension that builds your soul's strength and trains you to trust Love.

How do you judge yourself when you're unhappy? How can you satisfy yourself when there's a wall between what life is and what you want it to be? How can you improve your situation? What must you accept? What can you change? And how do you hold on as you watch your progress grudgingly play out? Like everyone, you have strengths and weaknesses. They're important because they determine your path in life. They measure your chances. A problem may not kill you, but it can make you think you're better off dead. Unfortunately, you can't just disappear. You're an eternal being and your responsibility to consciousness never ends. So God's support never ends. God will never let you fall so far that you can't get up. That's what life's about. You keep falling and you keep getting up. And you learn to love yourself a little more each time.

Even then your first thought isn't, "Just end it all!" You still want to win. You don't give up hope. You pray for a miracle. You're saying, "God, you gave me this problem. I can't take it anymore. Please help me." That's usually enough to get you back on track. God will intervene. God doesn't want you to suffer. God wants you to answer the hard questions of a difficult experience. God is always there but life is complicated. There are values to consider and other souls are part of it. You're connected. God wants you to find the connections that Love explains. A "successful" life has the same problems as a failed one.

Rich people worry about money all the time. They worry how they'll pay for their expensive lives. They worry who's trying to take their money from them. Is it the government, the economy, or some distant relative? They worry how they'll use their time when they don't have to work. Look at all the time we spend drinking. Everyone wants to escape. It doesn't matter how much your wine costs as long as it gets you drunk.

Self-aggrandizement is a lie you tell yourself. Its pretense is you're superior because your situation is better, however you define it. In truth, success is measured by how well you deal with your problems. It's how you apply Love to your problems. Life is more than survival. It's your values. It's how you weigh your opportunities. It's your focus shifting from survival to a life unrestricted by obstacles. Survival limits you. Life's necessities must be accommodated. It limits your self-respect to the compromises you'll accept, like how much you can afford for an apartment. It relies on conditions you can't control. You may need a doctor and not be able to afford one. You don't solve that by ignoring it. You have to find an option. You may have to wait longer for an appointment. You may have to find advice online. When survival is easy, you have tons of options. When survival is hard, you do what you can. Your choices reflect your values. Your self-respect depends on how well you live up to your values. It's not wrong to compromise yourself. It's only wrong to ignore yourself.

Question yourself. What's most important? How does it compare to what you have now? Is it owning a big house or is your reputation more important? Is it the distracted opinions of others or finding peace in your own thoughts? Where do you set the limits of responsibility? What are your expectations? How do they change with your moods? Do you share your last bit of bread with a stranger or argue with the dry cleaner over a stain on your shirt? How do you handle it emotionally? How do you handle it physically? How do you build on success? How do you cope with a failure? What do you do when your hopes are denied? What's the perfect answer to every question?

You feel uncomfortable when you see someone suffering, but most people expect someone else to fix it. Maybe you donate a dollar or you turn your head to avoid it. Reality is a shock. It's a human problem and it touches the conscious soul we share. It's the part that says, "Love one another." Maybe

SELF-RESPECT: THE SOLUTION TO UNSOLVABLE PROBLEMS

you're too busy or just numb from life's hardships. Maybe you think sharing your feelings is enough. But how can you turn away when you see it every day? There's plenty on your plate so how are you supposed to take responsibility for someone you don't even know? It's enough to stick your head in the sand as the endless tragedies create a sickening noise you can't turn off. It's the Information Age and, like it or not, you have to deal with it in a positive way that supports your self-respect. Ignorance was bliss, but you don't have that excuse anymore.

Your environment frames your self-respect. It's the same for everyone. Wherever you start, you try to do better. It's the foundation for your values. It's where you learn to get along with others. It's your priorities. You do everything you can but there's no limit to your self-respect. That's why you ask, "How do you combine self-respect with free will?" Free will changes things. It's important those changes reflect your self-respect. God designed free will to question your self-respect. It's how you balance your consciousness with God's consciousness. It's your invitation to the way Love works. It shows you; you can compromise and still be free.

A problem can be an opportunity. It depends on your point of view. It depends on your attitude. There may be no pleasure in it, but there's always a benefit. Look for it. You invest a lot in your problems so milk them as much as you can. Even when you compromise, you can only give away part of yourself. Your self-respect is God's expression, so you'll love yourself no matter how confused you are. Self-love is bigger than life. Staying in bed with a blanket over your head isn't hiding. It's a temporary answer to confusion. But it's not proactive. You're better off solving the problem than avoiding it. A problem is proof that you're ready for it. God has nothing to gain if you fail without a benefit. You can drown in self-pity or prepare for the future. It's up to you. But you have to want it. It's the lucid part of your consciousness that never gives up.

Your future is in your patterns. Patterns predict everything. Unusual events don't foretell the future. It's the everyday situations that repeat themselves and show you what to expect. You can prepare for a pattern. You know what's going to happen. It's not luck. It's not arbitrary. It's your soul's plan so you understand it. Once you accept it, it's manageable. Some people are successful gamblers and others lose every time. Gambling isn't for them no matter how much they like it. That door is closed for them. They're going to lose. But maybe they have a job they understand so well it's second nature to them. Whatever it is, they're comfortable with it. They're good at it. It's a pattern. It's God's gift. You have your patterns. You may be lucky or clumsy. So the clumsy person becomes a comedian and the lucky person starts a business. There's always a way to win when you respect who you are and respect your patterns.

Chapter 2
Self–Love

Self-love defines "finding yourself." It's not romantic Love. It's not Love in the gratification of owning something. It's Love for your self-respect. You find yourself when you satisfy your self-respect. You find confidence in your soul and a life you can be proud of. It can be confusing. In a world of conflicting opinions it's hard to know what to accept. But self-respect demands that you do what you think is right. It depends on you having sensible values. It's a process that helps you refine your priorities. It's how you mature. It matters because you're going to make mistakes. Practical mistakes aren't the problem. The problem is mistakes in judgement that come from an immature character. Practical mistakes can be fixed and forgiven. "That's life." the saying goes. It's not a problem if money can fix it. Character mistakes are different. They can take years to fix. And you have to be willing to work on it. Self-respect is a personal philosophy. Building your character is a lifelong mission. It's your soul's purpose. It's the foundation for your confidence. When you're conscious of it, you're in the game. The rest is just stuff.

Values are learned. You may be born with God's wisdom but applying it is the challenge. Much of your time is spent learning how. You have to respect society's rules. You're always questioning society with your self-respect in the balance. Caring about your self-respect proves your Love for yourself. Love and values go together. Judge your self-respect by how well you match your conduct to your values. It's the limits you'll accept. Self-love isn't interested in your beliefs. It's interested in God's Love. Self-love supports Love's kindness. Self-love is how you respect your connection to Creation. Once you have that, you're one with God. You can feel the Love in everything. When you open that door, the world is yours. Then you can put it to work creating more

Love. Creating Love is the measure of life. It's the Love you give and the Love you receive.

Self-love is the solution. It's not a series of achievements that lead you to a deathbed smile. It's not dying in peace. Self-love is always at peace. It's your conscious awareness of God. Conscious energy created the Universe. It created Love and the world you live in. Your connection to God is your connection to everything. Love it and it'll love you back. Your problems are respected. The solutions are created. But you don't always need a physical "solution." The concept of a solution is a judgment. Still, it's a logical part of the question. It connects you to God's possibilities. The material dimension depends on material means. But your soul's success is the Love you create. It has no need of anything else. Love is its own support. It has specific requirements. It cares about everything. The challenge is how to align your material values with your spiritual values. This you have to learn. This life teaches you. This God wants to know.

Problems test you. The answer is in your self-respect. Self-love is the success of your self-respect. It recognizes sometimes you make bad decisions. Life's purpose is to confuse you with endless opportunities. There'd be no need if eternal life was to lie in the sun and pick petals off of daisies. Life's confusing because God wants you to question it. Every moment is a challenge. So you need a point of view that defines right and wrong in any situation. It's your Love for yourself. It's what religions teach. Religious guidance isn't the answer to everything. Religions' purpose is to point to your connection to God. It's the "This is how you do it." answer that makes religions approachable from any point of view. Choose one you like or follow your own star. In their own way, they all do the same thing. They show you that better choices come from loving each other.

You live in two worlds. The physical world you know. The metaphysical world is the spiritual process of your soul's growth. The physical world can't answer metaphysical questions like, "Why were you born sick?" As soon as you think about it you're looking for the physical action that caused it. Every problem sets you on a path. Your soul knows what it's doing and creates scenarios that explore it. The best you can do is keep aiming at your goal. You probably won't like it. Nobody likes a problem, especially one not easily fixed. You identify physical problems having a metaphysical cause by their

SELF-RESPECT: THE SOLUTION TO UNSOLVABLE PROBLEMS

persistence. The solution doesn't react to logical efforts. It keeps coming back till you accept it. On one hand there's nothing you can do but let your soul do its work. The problem will go away when your soul's done with it. On the other hand, you can relax into your faith. Since there's nothing you can do you might as well trust God and find peace with it. A good way to judge your self-respect is by how well you tolerate the metaphysics.

Self-love guides your self-respect. It knows your limits and protects you when you're past your limit. You may be unhappy. There are things you want but you can't have. You may never sing in a rock band, but you can still feel the Love. You may not have the voice but you can enjoy the *feeling*. You can sing to your friends. You can sing in the shower. That's how you love yourself. That's how you enjoy the pleasure in being here. When you give yourself those *feelings*, that joy, that fun; you respect yourself. The problem disappears because you own its essence. It's not the selfie in front of the Eiffel Tower that makes your trip fun. It's the excitement in being there. Enjoy the experience of being yourself. Once your needs are met, it's your right to live your dreams. It's great when you see an opportunity. Life can be fun whoever you are. Opportunities are everywhere. But you're the one who makes it happen. So be brave. Suffer your doubts or enjoy yourself. Be smart but treat yourself well. Love yourself. Give yourself the experience. You can do anything even if you have to first learn how. You may not be able to afford that Mediterranean cruise but you can sit by the river on a nice day and have lunch. You can have a good time at a reasonable cost. That's how you love yourself. Walking your dog may be all you want. But that simple pleasure can lead you to an unexpected windfall, like being in the right place at the right time...and meeting the right person. Loving yourself is how you open life's doors. An opportunity is a responsibility. You have to respond to it and be sincere.

Everything is tolerable because you live it in your mind. You accommodate problems in your thoughts and feelings. Life is in your attitude towards it. It's what you'll accept. Life doesn't have to be "perfect" as long as you have what you need. Respect yourself. Demand what you need and accept the rest. That's why you laugh at an injury or are terrified when 10,000 people come to see you perform. It's impressive watching someone perform. They jump off a mountain, parachute down, and when they reach the bottom they have the biggest smile of their lives. They did it. They faced the danger. They enjoyed the thrill. They knew it was dangerous. You probably prefer a safe ride. Life's enough of a challenge when things go well. You don't need an additional danger. That doesn't mean you can't have the experience. You can feel the excitement watching a movie or in the controlled terror of an amusement park. You can have the excitement without the chance of hurting yourself.

Life is there for you. You can build a house or spend the day shopping. They both work because you feel the experience. They're opportunities to make good choices. Self-love is a positive experience. It's your consciousness questioning your welfare. You don't have to be smart. Use your common sense. Ask yourself why you like what you like and what could make it better. Look for the Love in it. It's more than a passing thrill. It's giving in to the glory of watching the sun set that makes you forget to take a picture. You don't need a fireworks show. Life is the greatest theater there is. It's playing your part instead of watching and watching instead of being bored. Everyone hates boredom. It's the antithesis of a soul's purpose. When I see a homeless person, I think it must be some mental confusion that led them there. Who could spend the whole day doing nothing and be happy? No one. That's why drugs are so popular. It's the easy answer to boredom. Loving yourself means caring about yourself. It's the Love you feel when you enjoy what you're doing.

Boredom burdens your soul. It ignores its inquisitiveness. You free it by doing what you like. You follow its lead. You care about yourself. You have to find your inner compass. That's why education is so important. It explains things. It's exciting finding something you like. It's a clear direction. The only rule is "participate." You have to do something. Life's exciting when you know what you're doing. Watching a game is more fun when you know the rules. It goes with every activity from meditation to parenting. You learn the relationships and apply what you learned. Your free will drives you forward. You're off the sidelines and into the game. Unfortunately, boredom can lead to convenience. It can dull your initiative. It's better to invest in a plan. It takes the same time. When you look for a fast solution, it's easy to miss something. It's the weak link that lets things fall apart. That's the cost of making convenience a priority. It's more important to do things right. Be patient. The process takes time.

SELF-RESPECT: THE SOLUTION TO UNSOLVABLE PROBLEMS

The solution to boredom is introspection; *questioning yourself*. It's considering your thoughts with your best interests in mind. It's a spiritual perspective that questions, "Are you happy?" and "What can you do to be happy?" If you're burned out by old routines; do something new! God's beauty is everywhere. See how it comes together. Trust it. Find your place in it. Find your Peace with it. It's a great way to cast off old habits and get back in the driver's seat. Whatever you do, enjoy yourself. Enjoy your pleasures knowing you're doing it for yourself. Like that you did it. You cared about yourself. Be proud of yourself. Accept your reward. Feel the elation. Joy is like a prayer. You succeeded and you'll succeed again. Whenever you do anything with Love for yourself, you respect yourself.

Contemplation is a good way to see yourself. Your thoughts aren't always visible. They hide in your habits. Many reside in your subconscious, close to your soul and hidden from consideration. So don't just react. See yourself and love yourself. Relax your mind. A calm mind is free and creative. It doesn't worry. It ignores the chaos, good or bad. It's defenseless. It trusts Creation. Pick something to think about. If your mind wanders, go back to that first thought. Separate the thoughts that intrigue you. Focus on them. Accept them without judgement. You know more than you think you do. Have priorities but accept your limits. You need an honest appraisal. Its only purpose is your well-being. Boredom is the perfect time to organize your thoughts. Dust off your old dreams. Don't concern yourself with the cost. You'll work that out. It doesn't cost you anything to think, and you have plenty of time. From there you can see your soul's wisdom. And it's not unusual for God to stop by with a kind word disguised as an inspiration.

Prayer is a commitment. It's your Love communing with God. It's not the fawning duty portrayed by religion. It's a welcome agreement. You ask and God listens, then God asks and you listen. Then you answer the questions together. It's your free will joining God's Love for Creation. God, the source of every thought you have, wants to know more. It wants to know your priorities. It wants to see how you weigh your values. You're not penalized for ignoring God. Life's just easier when you let God help. Prayer lets you take an active part in the solution. Your input is respected. Your Love is considered. God loves being part of your life. It loves your questions. The life you designed for yourself fascinates God, because you question your existence in the same way God questions its existence.

God is in your faith, trusting you're safe in its presence. And you're always in its presence. Love is everywhere. It's the comfort of a pleasant routine or the wonder in an adventure. It's finding Peace. Peace is a state of mind. Love defines it. It's more than satisfaction because it embraces God's presence. You feel God. Joy is your proof. You align with joy's certainty or fight with the chaos. Just ask a parent. Children are unpredictable. They decide for themselves what they like. God is orderly but it needs chaos to explore itself. Chaos makes sense because it creates opportunities. Chaos respects itself because it knows the result, the order of the Universe, is certain. Like a scavenger hunt, everyone meets back at the party to share their adventures. Life has ups and downs, but God only knows Love.

Love wants you to know everything. Love lets you add your perspective. Everyone has responsibilities, but you can create something just because you want it. You give life its meaning by sharing your personality. Self-respect is your perception of your value as a human being. Your consciousness guides you how to use it. It's not easy deciding your priorities when everyone's opinions are all over the place. Who do you trust? What's best for you? You have to trust yourself. It may be a new problem but your sincerity protects you while you sort through the options. You'll find the right answer. Love is a fair balance. To succeed in eternity you must respect Love. You can change your mind about the details. You're meant to. Details evolve. Creation moves quickly and you have to keep up. But as long as you're focused on a good result, there's no reason to believe you can't do it.

Most people aren't interested in details. They're not interested in life's interactions. They want simple answers. Complicated values confront them. They take work. And it's your responsibility. You feel it in your soul. It's in your nature. It's in your welfare. You know something's good or bad because you care about yourself. Problems don't solve themselves. You have to fix them. You have to change something. That's what your creativity is for. Your imagination is limitless so you can solve any problem. Clanking sounds under your car don't go away. They're a sign something needs attention. You have to face your needs. You have to face your fears about them. You have to

SELF-RESPECT: THE SOLUTION TO UNSOLVABLE PROBLEMS

accept that inconvenience is normal. That's how you respect yourself. Facing a problem is the way you solve it.

Life is about problems. It's the choices you make how to solve your problems. Some demand immediate attention. Others don't matter at all. Your choices matter because they promote your values. You have different priorities for every problem, but they all focus on what's in your best interest. There are spot-on-your-pants problems and having cancer problems, which shirt to wear problems, and crashed your car problems. Problems force you to question life for the best solution. You may have a hobby you love. Those are problems you like. They include the emotional stability dealing with failure as well as the physical problem in finding time to fix them. You always win because you like what you're doing. Whatever happens, you enjoy the experience. A motorcycle ride in a thunderstorm is a great story even though you hate it while it's happening. From the crib to the grave, you always need help. Fortunately, you're surrounded by Love and Love always helps.

Why does anyone need advice on how to love them self? If you're born with God's Love what else could you need? Life's purpose is confusing. It contains all the elements but not always in relationships you can use. So life becomes a question machine. It processes everything looking for solutions. You're a well-meaning soul, but life is a test. You learn something then you want to know more. You're looking for ideas you can trust. The problem is you might avoid something if it looks too hard. Survival is relentless whatever you choose. Even sincere people have different thoughts about fairness. Fortunately, there's God. God's Love is the answer, but you need to interpret it correctly. That's not so easy. The details may be incomplete or conflict with each other. Trust God has the answer. It's a tricky balance to respect everything. And you can only trust yourself to know what's important. You can ridicule religions, but Love is what they explain when they get it right.

Love is the solution. Love is the way out. God's mercy teaches you to forgive. When you forgive a mistake, the problem disappears. Forgiveness stabilizes the erratic energy in disappointment. The solution becomes a simple task, like tying your shoe. You had to learn how to tie your shoe and you have to learn how to tie up a problem. Relationships are tricky. They're emotional problems. They're an effort to equalize the free will in personalities. They're an effort to establish fairness in an emotional bargain. Everyone has to be happy with what they get. Everyone has to feel safe with what they give. It's the skill in balancing the primary energy in people. It's your trust that the Universe is working for you. Successful relationships represent a shared sacrifice and a shared benefit. Love supports everything so there really are no "problems", only the promise of better agreements.

Few have the opportunity to make a living through their art. Most people have jobs. Someone tells them what to do. They follow a plan to someone else's goal. They may be the manager or an intern but everyone works to get the job done. If you love yourself, you have to love how you make money. Everyone needs money. It's a necessity of civilization. Needs are described in financial terms. So self-respect includes being comfortable paying your bills. Next is making more money so you can have things that make your life better, like tickets to a show or having a family. You want work you enjoy, co-workers you like, and a nice place to work that's easy to get to. You're not designed to stare into space with an empty head. You're designed to think. You're designed to feel. You're designed to ask questions. You're designed to create wonders from the opportunities life gives you. So love your aspirations, respect your efforts, and enjoy the ride. There are always headwinds, but that's just nature.

Everyone has aspirations. Everyone wants something. So how do you reconcile when someone wants the same thing you do? You have to compete. You have to wake up early to be first in line. You have to work hard so your boss picks you for the promotion. Or you can sacrifice your character and cheat on a test or lie about a co-worker. There's a right way and wrong way to compete. Some people are born with a talent and it seems unfair they should have an advantage. But they compete against people who have the same advantage. There may be limited opportunities. In show business the competition is fierce and relatively few succeed to become celebrities. Celebrity is important. It proves their popularity and popularity is how they market themselves. It's their paycheck. But it comes with the burden of fame, a test of self-respect for anyone.

Professional sports are the same. Many want to play but there are so few jobs they have to compete just to be on a team. A star in high school doesn't mean they'll do well in college. All college players were great in high school but as they climb the ladder of success they compete against better players.

SELF-RESPECT: THE SOLUTION TO UNSOLVABLE PROBLEMS

Their success must be continually earned. It takes work to turn talent into skill. And their skills have to grow if they want to succeed. They have to keep practicing. They have to improve. They have to keep winning. When someone pays you to win, you either perform or you don't work. Eventually, someone with better skills is going to replace you.

Competition can be fair. It doesn't have to be cutthroat. Just accept there might be someone looking for an advantage who would cheat you out of your opportunity. Everyone wants to win and some people don't care about rules. You know because you make the same decisions about your own behavior. That's why people fight. They're happy to leave the competition bleeding on the ground. Then how do you respect yourself when you have to compete? How do you protect your opportunities? What's fair? Self-love balances your needs with your values. You don't have to push your way onto a crowded train. There's one coming right behind and another one after that. If you're afraid you'll be late, start earlier. You don't have to fight the world. Your creativity can solve any problem. You can have what you want and still respect Creation. Have faith. You'll get your fair share.

What if it's a matter of life or death? It may be inconvenient but no sensible person waiting in a hospital emergency room would deny the person having a heart attack should go before the one with a splinter. Competition is about reasonable choices. It's the time you spend watching TV competing with the time you spend playing with your kids. Your desires compete with your values. Everyone wants to win but you don't want anyone to get hurt, not if you have compassion. Frustration in a game of golf shouldn't damage your soul in the same way you'd kill an enemy in war. Your freedom's not at stake. Only a loving soul can accept war, regret it, and love themselves when it's over. A soul competes with its duty and the terrible choices it sometimes has to make. Love or murder is a bizarre competition but a natural conflict in human survival. Once your freedom is certain it's easy to be generous. Then you can question your sincerity and judge for yourself. Sincerity, thank God, is forgiven.

Competition can be good. It pushes you to do better. It helps you form alliances. It's a trade association or a life-long friendship. It's a natural commitment. A forest does better to survive than a lone tree on a hill. The world depends on natural alliances to maintain its massive balance through earthquakes, floods, and storms. They work together to balance its wild energy. You balance your nature in the same way. Your emotions constantly confront you: up and down, up and down, always looking for a happy medium. Life's not about owning the world. We achieve more when we help each other. The winner consoling the losers in the Olympic track finals doesn't eliminate the years of practice the competitors sacrificed just to be there. For the losers, their hope of victory is gone. They wanted to win. But they lost and only time can heal their feelings. For the winner, often by less than a second, their sacrifice is rewarded. But who knows what will happen tomorrow? Who'll be first next time? Who will the fates favor then?

Competition comes from the fear you won't survive. It's a lack of faith. Uncertain of success, you ignore God. You ignore God's Love. You want a guarantee. Love for you becomes a Love for things, a promise you can touch. It's how you keep score. You trust your desperation because you think you control it. It's a direction. You judge success by social standards because they're easy to compare. Society makes choices and you decide if you want to be part of it. It defines you because you let it define you. It may not be right, but in its own way it's fair. It's representative of your social experience. What's most popular? That becomes your proof. It's not the joy of competition where everyone helps each other accomplish a common goal. It's just winning. You're in or you're out and you want to be in. It's a problem because you might be tempted to sacrifice your self-respect for it. Eventually things work out and your self-respect will want its due. Then you'll pay and you'll pay gladly because it's for you.

Self-love is winning. A game can go either way, but in life you have to win. Fortunately, you define the *meaning* of winning. How you characterize your success is personal. It's not a question of how well you pay your bills. It's loving yourself no matter what. God creates the challenge and you solve it. That's how you win. You shouldn't judge yourself. Comparing yourself to a stranger is silly. Who's got the trendiest car doesn't matter. The trend will be somewhere else next year. It's like arguing which is the best college. There's no useful answer. The point is getting the best education for the career you want. Professionally, the prestige of a respected university may put an extra dollar in your pocket but you still have to perform. Some people have enough

SELF-RESPECT: THE SOLUTION TO UNSOLVABLE PROBLEMS

money for a thousand lifetimes. So what's the point of having more? When you have enough money to survive it's time for a challenge you can't buy.
Competition is personal. Whose neighborhood should be first to get their electricity back on after a storm? You might have to beg for it. You might have to shout for it. It's your comfort, your ability to get gas and groceries. But do you love yourself more for being first? Is the price you pay equal to what you achieve or is the cost too much for your self-respect? Would you trade your soul for a high priced watch? Some people would. Those things matter when you care about status. But they rarely measure up to your fantasies. It's better to focus on your character. Your consideration for others is important to loving yourself. When your self-respect comes first you'll always be happy with your choices.
The physical world is easy. You see how the pieces fit. You see the logic in it. Results aren't easy but your goals are clear and you know what you need. Time and effort bring success. You don't know everything but you'll learn. There are books and classes and the experience that comes with practice. You may be confused but it passes as you mature. Everything takes time. You become confident and learn to trust yourself. Then you can do what you like. But success is never guaranteed. You're up against competition so you have to trust your fate. Bad luck crosses everyone's path. You can have a great job when a health problem puts you in the hospital. That's life and life always wins. You can take all the medicine in the world but you can't command yourself to be healthy. It'll let you go when it's ready. You can take care of yourself though. You can have a positive attitude. You can be ready when your good luck returns.
Life is God's design. Love is God's support. Self-love reveres everything. God is the answer to everything. Your problems are God's opportunities. As crazy as it sounds, you volunteered. You wanted this. You win by making good choices. Your task is to balance the Love between you and the Universe. Everything competes so it's hard. You're always re-equalizing your priorities in the flux of nature's evolution. You have to figure how to evaluate it. But it's always changing. Love is the only stability you can count on. Who'll be first in line for the next electronic marvel? Who cares? But what does it mean when someone cuts ahead of you in line? What does it mean to suffer

someone's immaturity? When the world wants to pass you by, how do you treat yourself fairly?

Self-love doesn't keep score. It's not a plan. It's a feeling. It's not a measurement. It's your sensitivity to God's presence. You feel it in your Love for your kids and your delight when you smile at yourself in the mirror. Self-love is positive energy. It's healing energy. It's constructive. It holds your world together. It's the balance that encourages cooperation with every soul you meet. It's stronger than our differences. That's why extremes make the news. Loving each other is normal. People feel safe when they love each other. Anyone who rejects Love is the one out of balance. Love will never reject you. Love won't give up even when you fear it. The Universe will support you till you trust it...and never stops loving you. Love is inclusive and shares itself with everyone till they trust it too.

Life is hard for everyone. Having popular things doesn't guarantee you a happy life. You have to know what you want. You have to know when you have it. You have to know what's important and what does God think about it. It's easy to enjoy the ignorance that comes with distractions. Ignoring Love through distractions is how you avoid the introspection it takes to grow up. Instead, you create affectations to fill the void. Self-love doesn't need symbolic proof. It's your wisdom about life's values. It doesn't care whether you eat fast food or gourmet meals. It's self-respect based on God's virtue to love each other. You can deny it but you can't avoid it. The evidence is a tenacious responsibility that clings to your consciousness. Once you wake up your soul, it'll never be quiet again. It wants to help you. You have your values, but your soul insists on Love's values.

Self-love means caring about yourself. It's your desire to make good choices. You want to understand your life today, not in some unpredictable future. Even cooperation is a mystery. You're aligning with another soul's values. You have to adjust your priorities to make it work. It's like those survival shows on TV. Once they can sustain themselves they want to go home. They want to be where they don't have to worry about survival. They want the peace to do what they want and not scramble for their existence. Self-love drives them to do what they need to survive. Their self-respect is in what they're willing to do. On TV it's a game. In life it's your future. If you want a good life, then respect how you do it. When your values matter your character survives.

SELF-RESPECT: THE SOLUTION TO UNSOLVABLE PROBLEMS

Self-love respects consequences. It adores your hopes, and your efforts to fulfill your hopes. It likes problems because problems inspire you. Self-love is your connection to God's consciousness. It affects every thought you have. Your whole experience is involved in everything you do. No one is alone. Even the homeless have loved ones wondering where they are. To understand consequences, put yourself in a person's shoes. Feel their problems. What does their situation demand? What do they have to work with? Where will their choices lead them? "Opportunities and limits" are life's mantra. It's where Love finds balance in its effort to make a fair compromise. You can always respect yourself for being fair. Fairness and Love are the same.

You don't need anyone's approval to love yourself. You don't need anyone's permission. Love yourself regardless of opinions. There are many ignorant people preoccupied with a narrow view of life. It's normal. They have different concerns, and they're entitled to their beliefs. They think excluding others protects them. It's how they justify the values they respect. But we're not all Einsteins. God is your only judge. The principle of "us versus them" is easier to understand. Inclusiveness comes from Love's evolution. It's the eternal question. At one end is free will with everyone racing to be first. On the other end is the equality of human beings trying to survive. It's a pendulum with each cycle taking turns advancing human consciousness. It repeats itself regularly but rises with God's Love for Creation. Hatred comes from the differences we disrespect. It wants an advantage. Every part of Creation is an asset. Every human being matters. Unity demands the point at one end of the spectrum respects the challenge at the other end. Self-love is the peace between them.

It's easy to get lost in appearances. You worry how someone might judge you. You want to be part of everything. That's why everyone's crazy about trends. A trend does your thinking for you. It makes you the same as everyone. All you need is the right style and you're in. Trends are dependable. Since everyone's doing it, it must be okay. But you won't find peace unless you respect yourself, trendy or not. A rented tuxedo doesn't make you wealthy. It makes you feel wealthy. That's what you want anyway. You want to feel good. People judge you by the values that make them feel safe. Reasonable people expect you to share those values. Self-respect is personal so you have to be sure about it. The most important value is to love yourself. It's the only trend that never goes out of style.

A beautiful chair isn't always comfortable. You can make a gorgeous design that's a functional failure. The requirements are different. The basic principle of a chair is to be comfortable. You want something soft for relaxing or with a straight back for eating at the table. And for your desk you want it adjustable. Whatever it does, it has to be comfortable for its purpose. You want comfort regardless of what it looks like or how much it costs. The funny thing is comfort is cheap. The feeling you get sitting in the sun in your backyard is the same feeling you get lounging on the deck of a sixty foot yacht. The sun on your face is the same. Your relaxation is the same. It doesn't matter if it's a Long Island suburb or the French Riviera. You love yourself for that feeling. You don't have to attach it to wealth. Creativity is all it takes. There's always a park nearby. It just takes the effort to get there.

It's the same for people. You want good relationships. You want to trust the people you deal with. A rickety chair can break and you expect it, but a person can be broken inside and you can't see it. You can see when a chair won't support you, but how much pressure can a friend take when they're suffering in their thoughts? For the psyche, beauty is winning. Whether it's a pretty face or confident attitude; it *promises* success. When you're honest with yourself you know there's more to expect. Dependable people quit. Expensive clothes go out of style. Fancy cars break down. Self-love is always reliable because it prizes honesty. Self-love believes you should love yourself and everyone should love themselves too. But life can fool you. Someone can hide the rot and pretend it's not there. You need to know what's inside someone. You need to trust your support. Without that, there's only business.

If you love your character then having good character matters. Character knows life's a challenge for everyone. Character respects God's kindness. Shiny things don't need any thought. "It's beautiful. I want it." God is the beauty in everything. It's the singularity of Creation. Life connects you to everyone's needs. That's why people love money. You can buy whatever you like. You don't have to love it to have it. Wanting it for a moment then discarding it is acceptable. Feeding your desires seems like the answer to self-love because it answers God's call to be happy. It's logical but it's wrong.

SELF-RESPECT: THE SOLUTION TO UNSOLVABLE PROBLEMS

Life's impermanence prizes beauty because it's easy to achieve. You already have Love's beauty. You may not trust it, but it's part of the game. It's important because it may be the closest you get to knowing God. Love evolved from God's energy. Every physical form has it. The thing doesn't matter. The energy matters. Things are meant to provoke your free will. But your imagination is bigger than any bauble. Ownership isn't success. Love is success. Ask God if you don't believe me.

Self-respect is your guide. It's your sincerity. Life gives it contrast. Life's values and God's values seem different. Your priorities change day to day. What you trust at the moment depends on the circumstances. Your soul doesn't need the world's riches. Your soul needs Love. Self-respect is Love's beacon. You respect yourself so you expect to be respected. Love is the common denominator. There's never a problem when you respect self-respect, especially in others. You know what to expect. You know there can be a shared solution. Respect for others respects the Love each of us represents. Without it, everyone's on their own; alone and afraid. Even if a person doesn't respect themselves, it still exists for them. No one can be happy without self-respect. The problem is you can lose your self-respect to life's demands. Self-respect needs courage. Without mutual respect it's easy to be judgmental. Self-respect answers only to you. It's your Love for yourself. It can't be bought. It can't be trained out of you. It's greater than any suffering. You know it...even in your silence. The trick is, "How can you respect yourself when so much is against you?"

You don't want to intrude on anyone. Still, you may see yourself as better than others with no need to respect them. You may think they don't matter. There's an important benefit in respecting others. You become part of a community. You care about each other. You help each other. Treating people fairly should be part of every goal. But that's the limit of your responsibility. You're entitled to dream your dreams and make your dreams come true. Others may find your dreams useless. So go on without them. Consider them. Make a fair compromise but go for it. That's how mutual respect works with self-love. That's how you achieve your goal with your self-respect intact. Instead of forcing what you want down someone's throat, create an opportunity for them to participate. It's not easy. At times you'll butt heads. Some personalities are just contrary. That's the benefit of a community.

Others have their own dreams and their own way of doing things. That's when you negotiate. That's where you have to be creative to make a bargain and reap the benefit of the different ways people perceive things.

You don't give up your dreams because somebody says, "It'll never work." You may not have the answer right now. Compromise may seem impossible. That's why you're creative. You hear the word "obstructionist" when politicians point a finger and say, "Those people are obstructionists. They won't let the policy go forward and they haven't got a good reason." It's political name-calling. Of course they have a good reason. Politicians trade support to achieve each other's goals. The reason a person is an "obstructionist" is they feel they haven't received enough in political trade. In their eyes they want more to make an even deal. So the ball's in the other's court. Will they give more or be intransigent till they get more? As long as people are respected and treated fairly, as long as people put Love into practice, as long as people look for alternatives to make a better trade, they'll find a fair compromise. It's Love transformed, but it's still Love. It's working together, not forcing bad ideas on unwilling partners.

Some things you can't compromise. Religion and culture are like that. Negotiations require an equal alternative. But what's the alternative to God? What's the substitute for a cultural tradition a thousand years old? You wouldn't sacrifice your belief just to make a convenient agreement. You have to embrace your beliefs. You have to accept the differences God made in everyone. With a little effort, it can be one grand parade with every belief marching proudly while the rest of us cheer them on. God's purpose is in our differences. Differences create opportunities. That's how God explores Creation. We're all the same with exactly the same problems. Our joys are the same. Our hurts are the same. We just have different ways of seeing them. While God's Love is the same for everyone, humanity's interpretations are different. Cultures adapt and do their best with what they have. But that can cause conflict. One culture may want what the other one has. Faith needs practical answers. Faith is trust in Love, not trust in each other. Human beings have weaknesses, but Love never fails.

Wouldn't it be easier to subjugate a weaker culture? We've been suffering that delusion since time began. It's the human way to solve a problem. "They're different. I don't trust them. They're weak. I'm strong. I want what they have.

SELF-RESPECT: THE SOLUTION TO UNSOLVABLE PROBLEMS

I'll tell them what to do...or I'll force them." It ignores that survival is the same for everyone. Every culture's point of view comes from the desire to help themselves. Each one offers a different way to solve a common problem. But it's often simpler to crush them than do the work it takes to make an agreement. People love their cultures as extensions of themselves. It's easy to condemn the differences, but it's contrary to the opportunity God gave us all in free will. The opportunity in every individual increases all our opportunities. Unfortunately, when different cultures meet, fear reigns in the uncertainty of unfamiliar attitudes. Competition is always there. Whether it's a street gang or political movement, inside the group is Love and outside the group is fear. It's the limitation of a belief system that ignores God's purpose; to create more Love. Instead, it relies on group identity where rigid perceptions limit God's purpose.

What is a culture? It's a traditional pastime or the way you make a living. It's cowboy boots, blue hair, or a shirt with your team's name on it. It's being together and being yourself. Every society wants to do better so we created civilization to organize it as a living thing. Civilization is the most intricate concept ever imagined. It takes every personality and connects it to a single body. Everyone has a personal history. You make it what you like. You change it by changing your outlook. Your perception is the way you measure your self-respect. You probably see it as bits and pieces, but your soul sees a single experience. So respect everything. Care about everything. Safety is a concern for everyone. It could be you who needs the fire department next. The test comes in how you define your situation. Love is the unifier. Customs vary but Love is the same everywhere. Self-love is the same. Fulfillment is the same. Every culture finds a way to make life interesting. Each has its own point of view, its own artistic interpretation of how the pieces fit together. Their perception feeds your consciousness. Then your consciousness expands so Love can grow some more.

Self-love has no use for limits. It reveres your hopes. It pursues any path it deems beneficial. It sees possibilities in doing things differently. Imagination is your psychic dexterity. It's learning a language from a book or steadying a table with a book. The challenge is your free will. Different purposes create conflicts, but survival needs support. It's the principle of "You wash my back. I'll wash yours." There's always something to gain by working together.

There's always the small of your back you can't reach by yourself. You'll always need help and you'll always be asked for help. Whatever unfamiliar attitude you encounter, there's a good reason behind it guided by someone's Love for themselves. The question is, "How do you connect everyone's self-love with solutions that respect everyone else?" Self-respect is a challenge because you're always questioning what's fair and what you have to do to get there.

Human beings have common values. It means you can respect any culture. They may aspire to different things but fairness is the same. There are times you'll reject a social value when you feel it's an unnecessary burden, like when you speed through a stop sign on your way to the emergency room. Or you hold your responsibility so dear you'd risk your life, like first responders who risk personal injury to save a stranger in a dangerous rescue. Self-respect includes prioritizing your values when you're confronted by opposing goals. It's God's universal Love confronted by Nature's personal Love. Should you risk your life going into a burning building to save a pet which may not even be there? Life will throw you some doozies. You don't have to like it. You have to respect it. You have to respect the challenge; pray you make the right decision, and hope you survive.

Self-love invites examination. Keep asking yourself, "What's best when you have different answers to the same problem?" Keep questioning it. You want to be sure. You want to trust your confidence. You have to ask, "Do you have all the facts? Are you considering what's fair? Are you willing to compromise?" Love is your guide. You have to trust there's an answer that respects everyone and everyone will respect. You need the whole package, warts and all, with a positive view of the future. See what everyone wants; evaluate what everyone needs, then find a solution that serves *everyone*.

Sometimes you succeed and sometimes you'll succeed next time. The solution to an unsolvable problem is often in the future. A problem may not need an immediate answer. It trusts God will solve the problem when the time is right. Trust your persistence. Find comfort in your patience, not in the relief of an easy answer that doesn't solve your problem. You may have less control than you think. Life has its own way of doing things. But after Love, common sense is the only thing left. That or you gamble. Better to act wisely and examine things carefully. Don't be confused by your doubts. That's the point of the game, finding the hidden connections. It may not be what

SELF-RESPECT: THE SOLUTION TO UNSOLVABLE PROBLEMS

you expect but God isn't limited by your expectations. God's plan includes connections you can't see. You succeed by accepting reality, especially your spiritual reality. You were designed to question existence. It may take Eternity but you're not going anywhere. You have all the time in the world...literally. So enjoy Love, accept forgiveness, and create Love when you can.

Chapter 3
Free Expression

Self-respect defines free expression. You create it. Whether you do it reading a book, writing a book, or selling a book; you decide how you'll do it. In reading, you choose a feeling you want to experience. In writing, you decide the idea you want to communicate. In selling, you compete for survival. Satisfaction drives you. That's the point. Creativity helps you find your satisfaction. Your physical presence, including your attitude, is how you negotiate life. Are you strong enough to lift that box? Your mind calculates the obstacles. Is it too heavy? Is it too bulky? Your creativity can change those circumstances. You can use a hand truck or get someone to help. You're always asking, "How can you make your life better?" Then you do it.

There's no limit to your imagination. You start where you are then imagine where you want to be. It's impossible to be a blank slate. You're constantly questioning your thoughts. Everything matters in relation to what you want. You don't need a pretty tree when your priority is wood to build a house. Beauty comes in all shapes and sizes. Pretty forests and pretty neighborhoods are both important. The question is your priorities. Sometimes the view is more important and sometimes a place to live is more important. Life's a jumble. You give it order through your priorities. Creation is God's wonder but without your questions God can't explore it. God is pure energy. You give it clarity because you have free will and you have an identity. Plus you have imagination. The way you create an identity gives God its vision. The trick is you have to balance Love with what you create. Your questions and your questions about the answers give God a fresh look at Creation while Love keeps everything together.

Survival is the height of self-awareness so self-respect depends on you staying alive. Life tells you how well you're doing. It signals discomfort when you're hungry, pain when you're hurt and misery when you're disappointed. Your comforts do the same thing on the other end of the spectrum. They signal well-being when things go your way. You're not a blob in the Universe. You're not a mysterious ghost. You're a creative human being, whole with God, and continually engulfed in massive streams of information. It's confusing, impossible to avoid, and you're responsible for it. And it increases with every question you ask. So your best choice keeps changing with the rhythm of Creation. Eek! What are you going to do about it?

Ask God. God is there. Life is there. Consciousness is there. So how do you join them together? You have to think creatively. If one thing doesn't work try something else. You have everything you can imagine and when you talk to someone else, you have everything they can imagine too. Every possibility is available. In its own way, everything is divined but it's up to you to make it real. You're supposed to question things. Maybe you first have to acquire a skill before you build your dream. There weren't always space rockets. People worked hard solving the engineering problems and today we have space travel as an attainable goal. Or it could be as simple as practicing your guitar every day to build a career in show business. That goes for anything. Life takes time. Fortunately, you have as much as you need. Whatever you want you can have if you're patient and work at it. That's how life works. You grow into things. There's no rush. Immaturity is a bother but impatience ignores Nature. It ignores getting your values right and not racing past something important.

Creativity is personal. It's who you are. You can share it or not. You express yourself through your creativity. You can be the "oddball" or "run with the crowd." And you don't have to justify it. In fashion, there's a lot you express in the nuances you choose. The tilt of your hat or a political pin may be all it takes. Flashy or low key, there's no right way to express who you are. You have to feel good about yourself. You have to be with people who accept you for who you are. When you look in the mirror, your responsibility is to yourself. Still, you should be appropriate. Wearing a red hat isn't suitable at a church funeral. Basic black expresses the right attitude. It's a respectful response to a social event. In society, you adapt to the situation or you don't belong there. You respect yourself but you also have to respect the community. It doesn't take much effort. You do it for Love. No one is asking you to donate a kidney.

SELF-RESPECT: THE SOLUTION TO UNSOLVABLE PROBLEMS

You're meant to be creative. Just don't intrude on anyone else. Self-respect has rules. Some jobs, like the military, have a unique regimen but it's your choice to be part of it. Strict rules may be needed to do a job safely, like in the airline industry. That's the essence of self-expression; to respect yourself *and* your responsibility to others. Sometimes your imagination is more important, like how scary you can look for Halloween. You just don't want to traumatize the kids. You can go unkempt around the house, but when you're out in public you should look presentable. How you present yourself is a sign of what people can expect from you. A fair society will give you room to express yourself. Social rules help everyone. "Live and let live." You want life to be as fair as possible. Everyone has their own way of doing things. If you have a nice voice, no one's going to fault you for singing on the train. It just requires some creativity to accommodate anyone who might not be in the mood for a song.

While self-respect is personal, society makes rules that protect everyone. You may think your free expression comes first, but what if someone else has the same idea and their free expression conflicts with yours? It happens every day. Civilization supports fairness. When people can't agree, laws enforce a compromise. Wherever people interact, there's always the possibility someone will cut in line. Laws set the limits of free expression so everyone can be respected. That's why people like walls; just the ticket for someone who wants to study without being bothered by the neighbor's kid practicing the saxophone.

You need society. Social systems make life easier. It's unlikely you'll find a drugstore in the desert. An aboriginal culture can live off the land. They've had a thousand years' experience. They rely on their tribe. Their environment is hard in the best of times. You have to know what you're willing to sacrifice. What does society ask of you? Life has a different answer for each of us. You could be a hermit in the woods. You could live the independent, rural life. You could enjoy the balance of the suburbs. Then it comes full circle where people hide in the congestion of the cities like they're back in the woods. You decide where you feel most comfortable. Every place has plusses and minuses, but you know who you are wherever you are.

Your free expression is always "on" so you have to control it. It must be focused. It shouldn't be impulsive. It shouldn't be overly considered. It's a balance. You have to discipline yourself to work with Creation. Everything has its own free expression. Everything wants to benefit itself. It's all one thing so Nature must be respected. Every identity follows its nature. Sometimes it's your turn and sometimes you have to wait your turn. Times change, so you have to protect yourself while the world adjusts. Society depends on you accepting its way of doing things. If everyone does whatever they want whenever they want, the social contract will fail. Communication ceases. Civilization requires that everyone's opinion be respected. Everyone needs to know what everyone else wants so society can include it. You have to find a way to connect with it. It's the respect Love brings to every thought. You're a social animal. Unless you can live without food and shelter you'll need help. We help each other by making things others can use. Then we trade. You don't have to live ten to a room or alone on an island. Besides those extremes, there are many ways to live your life. You might like the tumult of a big city filling your head with ideas. Or you may prefer the solitude of a small town where your thoughts have a safe place to surface. Do whatever you like. There's no right or wrong as long as you respect yourself and live by the Golden Rule. You're not bound by your decisions. Try what looks interesting then change when you find something better. That's how your self-respect grows.

You grow with your responsibilities. You could be at a company with a thousand workers or it could be just you working from your kitchen table. Even when you prize your independence there are times you need help. An important part of self-respect is getting along with others. You have to help those who need you and ask for help when you need them. It's trading Love. "I need you to care about me. How can I care about you?" It would be great if everyone had a clear mind but most people are hanging on just trying to survive. Life is a handful and your job is to respect yourself and love the people around you despite it all. You have to feel it in your heart. That's your motivation. The extraordinary thing is you do it all the time. Most problems aren't as bad as they seem. They're expectations. You're always learning, but you need a mature foundation to appreciate it. You need positive values. You need advice you can trust and fixable mistakes that reveal your immaturity in the same way an inappropriate fart teaches you humility.

SELF-RESPECT: THE SOLUTION TO UNSOLVABLE PROBLEMS

It's the difference between self-respect and following a trend. You're the judge. Advertisers have you gazing out at the ocean standing by the condo pool with a glass of wine in your hand and your significant other knowingly smiling you've arrived. But you don't need a condo to get drunk and there are plenty of public beaches. It's not easy having goals. It's easier to imitate someone else's goals. You mimic someone's values because, right or wrong, it's a clear direction. But think about it. They have their own interests in mind. Maybe they're mimicking someone else. You have to respect yourself and choose the opportunities that support *your* interests. You have to question yourself. You have to know what you want. As a child, the candy store had all sorts of treats. If you didn't like one, you took something else. No matter how old you are, you're still looking for the best treats. Today it's a new car or a hug from your kid. Copying others is great when you don't know any better. It's a silent recommendation and you're not bound by it. Happiness is where you find it, so be honest with yourself. When you trust your own wisdom, a loving world will support you.

Free expression is the way you solve problems. First you imagine the solutions. Then you pick one and hope it works. It may be easier to have someone pick one for you. You may lack the confidence. Maybe you have trouble picturing your goals. When you're young it's wise to follow a teacher. When you're grown it's wise to hire professionals. They've already done the work to have the answer to your problems. Free expression believes you can solve any problem when you set your mind to it. It takes effort. It takes time. It's not how wild you can be. It's not your art or your lifestyle. Free expression is the freedom to live your life the way you want, whether it's driving a truck or hunched over a microscope. It's living your attitude and loving your life. It's your involvement in what you like. It's how you prepare for the changes to come. It's who you are when you feel good about yourself.

That's why people like drugs. Drugs rewire your feelings. They're comforting. But they can also short circuit your consciousness. They can release your free expression when you can't do it consciously. They can calm you down or pep you up. People depend on social conformities to feel safe. That's why people like drugs. They're like a psychic key. They allow you the freedom of not caring, at least for the moment. Social behavior needs control. That's how we love each other. Drugs bring relief from having too much control.

But they can also lower your resistance to the limits that protect you. That's why medical professionals are important. They understand when the drugs aren't helping. They know what might work better. Drugs can subdue your preoccupation with your fears. They can put a positive image on the face you show the world. It's important because that face is the way you convince the world to trust you.

Freedom asks you to respect what you're doing. It asks you to know *why* you're doing it. It's okay to have a different face for each situation. It's important to express yourself appropriately. Sometimes you're the demanding leader and other times you're the compromising peacemaker. Free expression isn't the right to intrude on someone. Every society has a measure of respect it expects. If you don't accept it, bad things can happen like being fired, divorced, incarcerated, or the focus of a lawsuit you'll lose. While disrespect may include elements of free-expression, it's not free-expression. It's superiority. It ignores the social contract. Human beings are meant to work together...not destroy each other. Free expression makes it your choice as long as you give everyone else the same choice.

Greed causes most conflicts; greed for money, power, or attention. It's like the environmental movement. Part of the problem is the developed nations realize they've gone too far exploiting the world's resources. Now they tell the developing world not to make the same mistakes while they've already benefitted from them. They achieved a good life but left terrible scars on the world, often on someone else's world. Now they tell the developing world to stop working on their prosperity; that they shouldn't even use *their own* resources. They tell them to stop mining and foresting for the sake of "the planet." But everyone wants a good life and their kids are hungry now. Resources are important, but is a beautiful vista more important than feeding your family? It's a tough compromise, but Love will find the answer if we consider everyone fairly.

Life isn't measured by healthy societies ignoring the ones who helped pay for it. They're measured by sharing the benefits of successful societies. It's helping the less fortunate educate themselves for a better life. Struggle may be all they've known. Their free expression is to use whatever's at hand. Their self-respect is to survive. Like everyone, they crave the freedom in their souls. People will always love God and pray for justice. Even in their desperation

SELF-RESPECT: THE SOLUTION TO UNSOLVABLE PROBLEMS

their self-respect is pre-eminent. It's easy to judge someone, but life can push you beyond your abilities. Think road rage when you're the one who's upset. One day a stranger makes a mistake, the next day you make the same mistake. Every day is different but the issues are the same. You're always making decisions that prioritize your self-respect.

Free expression is your right. It's not toying with Nature. It's the way you survive. It's the way God gave you to support yourself. It's how you solve your problems. Once you achieve your needs, it's your insight into life's possibilities. It's how you live God's experience. Your talent is reverse engineering. You ask yourself why God made things the way they are…and what you can do with them. You can do anything. You can sail the Pacific or change your hairstyle. It's what you do when you feel safe. It goes back to when you first learned to climb out of your crib. You felt the freedom. A point comes when a "safe" life isn't enough. So you get married or change careers. You hope the challenge will nurture your aspirations despite the risk. Risk is important. It's how you question life's possibilities and explore their potential. It's how you learn right from wrong. It trusts your free expression will enjoy God's support.

Without you, freedom has no purpose. Your creativity gives it a purpose. It's your experience and you can do with it whatever you like. It's also your responsibility because it answers to your soul. Your free expression mimics God but with a difference. You have your happiness in mind while God explores Creation's possibilities. God wants to know why you chose what you did. The only rule God has is to love everything. That's why it's wise to ask, "What's Love's role here?" Was your priority to love yourself at the expense of someone else or sacrifice yourself unfairly? Regardless of what happens, did you make the right choice? Did you skip your child's recital to work on a project that wasn't needed? You live by your choices. There are no do-overs. The moment is gone. All you can do is respect your regret and try to do better next time. Your soul accepts this but your humanity struggles with it. You have many problems but your goal is always the same; to answer life's questions. So let Peace be your guide and forgive your mistakes. That's also your soul's job because you deserve Love too.

Free expression is your creativity. It's the answer to every problem. Everyone can do it. But even a technologically advanced extraterrestrial can't do it quite like you. You're not a collective organism like an ant colony. You have no master soul like plants and animals. In this Universe you're individually you, a unique possessor of free will and all its possibilities. Only when you express yourself can you respect yourself. Anything else, like a bad marriage or hated job, will leave you disappointed. You can change things by being creative. You can find a better way. You can challenge the consequences. That's the beauty of a hobby. It's personal. It gives you the peace to enjoy an experience you like. It's separate from survival. Its disappointments are acceptable because you like what you're doing. Like the saying goes, "A bad day fishing is better than a good day at work." Freedom feels good. The "good life" advertised in the media appears as luxurious escapes; endless leisure that ignores responsibility. But a fat bank account doesn't guarantee you good health. Healthy habits support your good health. Free expression must be a healthy habit because it's the way you respect yourself.

You're always making adjustments. Your free expression balances the world's changes. Everyone has free expression and it's probably different than yours. This could mean a conflict. People live in a compromise of appropriate behavior. Every life has its own demands. We all have bills to pay. You understand it because it's your life too. You know how to respect people because you know how you want to be respected. You trust people because you know what to expect. We're all the same. You know what they want because you want it too. You learn how to share without sacrificing. Love is never a sacrifice. You don't want anyone intruding on you and you don't want to intrude on them. It's common sense not to put a pig farm where people live and the smell is a nuisance. A home should be a peaceful place. However you measure it; free expression starts with your self-respect. It only asks that you trust it.

Free expression can be spontaneous so you have to pay attention. You don't want to lose yourself in a wild emotion and be inconsiderate. Appreciate who you are. You don't want to muck up your life to the point it's irreparable, like going to jail or having kids you can't afford. So how can you be free and sensible at the same time? Life blesses you with success when it's right for you. Blessings lessen life's burden but they can't solve *all* your problems. Character issues are different. Every decision you make questions your character. It can be a wild river so you have to control it. Your character is

SELF-RESPECT: THE SOLUTION TO UNSOLVABLE PROBLEMS

what you decide it should be. It's important because it aligns you with God's consciousness...Love. It takes effort and the Universe will react. Fortunately, God forgives your confusion. Your life is defined by the elements of character you respect. Character is how you express Love. It's the values you give it. You're always asking, "What's more important?" Your soul doesn't care how much money you make. It cares how much Love you create.

Life makes choosing your priorities a job. You'd rather lose yourself in life's wonders or be amazed by the sights in some science fiction movie. You love new ways of seeing things. Your practical side tries to remember its purpose. You still have to respect your values whatever you do. The problem is sorting through the information. That's why aggregating websites with all your choices in one place are a life-saver. They eliminate much of the work. Think of all those travel websites. Is the price more important or is it the location? Is it the attractions or the food? You have choices you weren't even aware of, but the internet puts them all in one place on your computer. Then your free expression reduces it to the only thing that matters...your happiness. Eureka! It's the end of the mystery and the answer you were hoping for.

Your job is to manage your life. So you have self-control. Free expression gives you choices. Self-respect is in your priorities. It's the chaos of balancing your values like you're riding a skateboard over cobblestones. It's a rough ride. Free expression is your stability. It feeds the joy in you. You can race down a hill or avoid it altogether. You do what makes you happy. Self-respect respects the balance. It's what you want and what you're willing to pay for it. You'd like everyone to love each other but self-preservation makes you wary of human nature. God made loving each other a challenge. You're supposed to make judgments about your relationships. You're supposed to ask, "What happens when this person is confronted by something they can't avoid? What will they think is most important then?" You're supposed to love some people with your life and everyone with your soul. Love has many expressions and you learn from them all.

It's nothing to feel bad about. It's what God does. God explores its existence through Love. The perfection of Paradise is for Paradise. Here Love's perfection is a question. You have to decide what you'll do with it. What should you do for yourself and what should you do for others? Life's challenges are Love's game. But the pieces don't move the same for each player. Turn away for a minute and the whole board changes. First you're playing checkers then you're playing chess. Your goal is to win. But, unlike a game, you want to win without your opponent losing. It's like being on the same team but competing for the same position. You have to find a way to respect yourself and love yourself while you love everyone else too.

Be who you are in your thoughts. It's the person you want to be. It's someone you like. It's the life you aspire to. Be positive. Be confident. Don't be a slave to social trends. Don't burden yourself with other people's opinions. Fitting in is great as long as it respects your values. Your life is to figure a fair compromise between your values and the values you find in every relationship. You want to feel good about yourself. The challenge of the "blank slate" you wake up to each morning is in the way you make your day. It's your soul's decision on the problems you'll accept. You evaluate your environment, focus on your priorities, and mold them into what you want. Then you hope it takes you where you want to go.

Free expression can't be satisfied by an old routine. Routines are helpful but bound by their limits. You don't want a good routine to become a bad habit. Things change. Revise your routines to keep up with them. Free expression nurture's your creativity. You don't have to wear the same thing every day. You can change colors or wear different jewelry. That's why people travel. They enjoy seeing different cultures negotiate their unique environments. What are their routines? Routines are the perfect answer to boring tasks, like walking the same way to work every day. It may be practical but it can dull your inquisitiveness. Free expression can improve a routine. Brushing your teeth is perfect for a mindless routine. You just don't want to be a machine about it. Ask yourself how brushing your teeth could be better. Respect it. How would you do it? When you buy toothpaste, look for one that offers you tartar control or a whitening agent. Look for a better toothbrush. That's how you breathe life into a tired routine; by letting your free expression change it. Life evolves and you should evolve with it.

Challenge your creativity. Make it work for you. Explore your imagination. Examine your curiosity. Define life in different ways. Demand common sense from your ambitions. Respect your presence and the free will God gave you. Humanity's evolution is your path. History will show you everything. Free expression starts in your consciousness. Every moment you question your ability, whether it's taking out a splinter or a way to be a better parent. With your answers, your life improves. Your values mature. You have an ambition so you make a plan. Then you work at it and change your life. You don't have to be an artist to think like an artist. You may not have the talent but it's fun to wear a crazy hat. That's free expression too. That's being human. You create to survive. You don't live by stumbling on opportunities. You're not a foraging bird. You can see Nature's opportunities when you use your imagination. It's how Love guides your soul to restructure your environment. Don't accept the world as it is. Make it what you can imagine.

Free expression helps you adapt. Your survival depends on it. You start with an observation. You ask yourself, "What's that? What's it doing? Why does it do that? How does it do it? Could you change it to do something else?" You use your ingenuity and interact with it. You move it. You twist it. You add something. You take something away. Maybe it works. Maybe it doesn't. Maybe it needs more tinkering. Technology evolves and you try again. There was a day someone realized they didn't have to wait for the seasons to change to bring the next harvest. They could engineer it. So they built machines to make the work easier. They nourished it with fertilizers. They irrigated it. They killed the pests that ate the crops. They respected Nature's need for regeneration and rotated the crops. They increased the output so more people could live from it. Free expression doesn't surrender to Nature's chaos. It looks for the meaning in it. Nature is practical. It's good at taking care of itself. You may not see everything, so don't be in a rush to change it. With Nature, a mistake can take a long time to fix. You have a rightful place here. Free expression is your God-given ability but you live side by side with Nature. Respect it and you'll find a good partner.

Can you go too far with your free expression? Yes. You have to do it properly. It's limited so you have to know what you want. Human beings need their imagination to survive. It's like the furry coat of a winter fox or an aloe leaf soaking in the Sun's rays. Besides your creativity, you're born with few protections. Nature is harsh so you have to make the best of it. Human nature is especially harsh so you need creativity in your relationships. You're constantly adjusting to people who are constantly adjusting to you. Free expression is emotional. You need sympathy and perseverance. You need values and priorities. Plus, there's the jumbled community of human beings all living their own free expression. Relationships are complicated. Growing up can take you twenty years just to know what you want. That's Nature. If you're too cold then move somewhere warm. Self-respect means you're not a slave to Nature. You can change it or change your relationship to it. What seems like a lack of protection is really your freedom. Nakedness is your opportunity to wear whatever you like. The only thing self-respect answers to is your values. Loving values are your protection and Nature knows it.

Self-respect supports your values. It's what you believe are your responsibilities. It's what you expect of yourself and what you expect from others. When you balance those, you have a good basis for your free-expression. Reasonable expectations may not be realistic. Solutions affect us all differently. Every outcome has a different benefit. That includes your responsibility to God and your respect for the community of souls…human beings and all the other conscious entities. Why do we pay so much attention to feeding the homeless on Thanksgiving when you know they're hungry every day? It's a natural conflict when you have to feed your family and pay the bills each month. And how should you value your creativity? You'd never want to sacrifice that. It's the essence of your being. That's why people like working for themselves and doing things their own way. You just don't want anyone to suffer. You want life to be fair. Unfortunately, some people can't manage their lives.

Love is your priority. You define what it means to you. So question your values. Be honest with yourself. You walk Love's tightrope with every thought. But how do you keep your balance when the environment keeps changing? It's hard to believe you control it. And it's disappointing when you lose hold of it. Disappointment feels bad, but you don't want to sacrifice your self-respect to self-pity or self-aggrandizement. That'll make things worse. So do the right thing and hope for a good result. But where's the sign that says, "This is the right thing?" You can only trust your soul's sincerity. You don't need a fat purse or a high IQ. You need realistic values and the belief that you'll make the right decision when you set your mind to it. You can avoid a decision but you can't avoid your responsibility to make that decision. Don't wait to respect yourself when you're perfect. Perfection is luck. It's in your mind not your soul. Your soul is always perfect. Respect yourself for trusting Love then perfection will be what you make it.

SELF-RESPECT: THE SOLUTION TO UNSOLVABLE PROBLEMS

Free expression makes you a real person. It's more than wearing the perfect shoe that speaks exactly who you are. It's more than a work of art illuminating your psyche with perfect understanding. Free expression is the joy in your free will. It's the value in your creativity. It's your wisdom and self-respect. You have a mandate to question the world. You can be safe and avoid the risks or risk everything and challenge the mystery. Will you fall off the mountain or find your answer in trusting God? Will you gain wisdom in the experience, win or lose? Free expression is the solution. Free expression aligns with your self-respect because it supports your values. Love's priority is your self-respect. It's your unique approach to Creation. God is conscious energy. Creation explains it. Love joins it together. When you trust Love, God supports your free expression.

Don't worry you'll go too far. God is everywhere. God is always present. God is always aware. God knows everything about you. You're not limited by Nature. You're only limited by the way your imagination works with Nature, your free will. You have unlimited choices. Your imagination makes everything useful. You want the comfort of your self-respect despite the crush of society telling you what to do. It's confusing. There's so much resistance. It's the challenge of living with diverse opinions. It's the character skills you have to learn. It's the tolerance you have to master. God's Love guides everything including your free expression. People get along when they're free. Some rush and others meander. But Love is how you respect everything and respect yourself in the bargain.

You have opinions about others and they have opinions about you. Since you don't know everyone you judge them by their affiliations; their culture, politics, sexuality, and activities. You may like their attitude. It's who you'd like to be. So you learn more about them. Then that group's values become your values, whether it's a criminal gang or a religious crusade. You want to know their history because it traces the evolution of their goals. It's how you'll live if you join them. Everyone's the same. We all have abilities and disabilities, joys and sorrows. We've won and we've lost. The details change but they change the same way for everyone. Life's predictable. It's how you prepare for the future. Everyone's looking for a dependable balance. You can be the life of the party or the wallflower. It's your choice. Just don't hide from yourself. Take the initiative. Who you are reflects your soul's effort. The details matter. You matter. You're a unique individualization of Creation. It's your free expression. It's your opinion of yourself when you have no limit. Your Peace may be personal but we all need you to live it.

You'll solve the riddles. You'll balance your purpose with Nature and honor God while you do it. God's consciousness is the unity of Creation. It's God's Love for itself. Even if you renounce God, you're always part of its consciousness. Denying God is simply another experience. Believe it or not, you always have God's support. You're designed as a co-creator. Belief doesn't make you part of it and it's impossible to quit. Your existence is your membership. Your purpose is to explore your free expression in every variation including denial. Love keeps the balance. Look at all the questions you ask. What do you want? You can see all the parts, but how can you work with them when they're already together? Making revisions is your job as co-creator because God's already connected everything. You're really asking, "How can you *redo* it to match your free expression?"

You were born to Love's perfection. Despite the difficulties, Love protects you and guides you. It's exercise for your soul. Life has to be challenging or why bother? It's designed that when you realize it, you wouldn't have it any other way. That's why it's important to see yourself as an eternal being. Life's hardships are your teacher. Life can jump out at you like a toothache or be something you quietly nurture like a life-long friendship. Every experience is a chance for you to grow. Each experience adds depth to your personality as you incorporate it into your being. Each experience increases your awareness. You have a responsibility to choose a path through Eternity. Your problems are a custom fit. Your soul sees them as opportunities. Free expression makes you choose between your material values and your spiritual values. Your job is to weave them into a loving personality. That's why life needs your sincerity. Everything matters. Right or wrong often hangs by a single thread, a yes or no answer that changes your life forever. It's valuable because it's your investment in Eternity.

Life is measured by the Love you create. Your reward is the joy you feel. It's the success of your self-respect. It's meeting the challenge of your humanity. You have to balance your comfort with your Love for God. That's how you win at Love. It knows when you have enough and doesn't let you get lost in routines that keep you asking for more. Love can never be a routine.

SELF-RESPECT: THE SOLUTION TO UNSOLVABLE PROBLEMS

It's always a conscious choice. Love is free expression's perfection. It's your eternal soul embracing your daily life. You have to love yourself no matter what. It's your trust in hope despite the obstacles. Don't ignore your struggles. Just don't empower them. Don't identify with them. Don't suffer them for the pleasure of friendly sympathies. Have a positive attitude. Free expression has to be positive or you'll lose yourself in justifications. Free expression is like a beloved pet. When you lead it, it'll love you.

Free expression is your ability to think creatively...and then make it happen. That's why oppression is frustrating. You need your freedom for your soul to thrive. You build your life on it. It's the way you love yourself. It connects you to everything. It's your beliefs. What you imagine you create. It's your attitude towards life. Your soul may be eternally wise but your life depends on your beliefs. Success comes when your beliefs mature. Mature beliefs include Love. Your maturity judges you. When you embrace it, you do well. Personal aggrandizement becomes unimportant. In maturity, Love blooms despite your old realities. Your maturity is intimately conscious of you. It cares about you and has the experience to help you. But you have to know what you want. More than anything, God loves your confidence. You don't have to be right. You have to be honest.

Beliefs drive your free expression whether you're a solitary toll-taker or a renowned fashion designer. You live in the culture of your times. It's your responsibility because that's where you are. It's how your self-respect expresses your creativity. Love supports everyone in every culture. You have to find a way to express yourself that gives you peace. It could mean being a foster parent or having a common hobby like collecting baseball cards. It's beyond culture. It's your being. It's how you balance your creativity with your social responsibilities. Love is your soul's culture. It's impossible to avoid. You're one with Creation so consider everything. Knowing you're part of it should relieve any doubts. Self-respect is the same for everyone. Everyone's looking for a happy balance where their life is manageable. Free expression is the courage of your creativity managing itself. It trusts God is your partner. It makes Love practical. Faith defines free expression because it trusts God's role in everything.

Free expression takes courage. You have to be brave in the way you answer life's questions. Free expression connects you to God. You have an expression that's uniquely you. With God's help you designed it. It's your soul's plan. It won't ask for more than you can handle and supports your spiritual goals. Without spiritual goals, life is meaningless. You won't be asked for an explanation of the Universe. What's important are the "right or wrong" choices you make every day. Free expression is your talent to solve problems your own way. Everyone does it. It's your responsibility to consciousness. Respect your contribution. It's real. Free expression isn't an artist's eye for color. It's the values that define you.

God wants you to trust yourself. God wants you to trust your free expression. It only asks that you love the experience. Free expression works through Creation. It connects you to everything. It puts you everywhere. It's God's way of saying you're not alone. Creation is God's answer to consciousness. God gave you free expression to explore the twists and turns. With God's guidance, you can do anything. Your successes are your pleasures and your mistakes are your education. From that perspective, everything's a benefit. People judge you by their beliefs, but you judge yourself by your values. You know your priorities. You know what they do for you. You know your limits. However stressful your life is, it's yours. Sincerity frees you from judgment. Just pay attention and do your best. God trusts you enough to give you free will. That alone should impress you with yourself. God's pleasure is seeing what you do with it.

Chapter 4
Survival

Self-respect begins with your survival. You successfully negotiate life's demands or you don't survive. As a baby you realized your discomforts and cried to let the world know you needed help. You were hungry or wet and needed attention. You didn't have the maturity yet to take care of yourself. Human beings are born dependent on others.

It's more than the need to feed yourself. You have to learn to teach yourself. You have to learn to identify your needs. You have to find an answer to your needs. In the same way your physical needs reflect your body's character, your values reflect your soul's character. Consciousness is your independence. That sense of presence gives you the ability to change things. Awareness is your natural environment. It's where you focus on your purpose. Good health promotes your growth. It's the equilibrium of a reliable foundation that supports your adventure. Think how hard it is to make a decision when you're tired. The good news is you can do well, but you have to improve yourself. The question to keep asking is, "How can you be a better person?" As trivial as it may sound, the answer always comes.

Your mind, body, and soul are inseparable. Your consciousness mixes them together then sorts them into new ideas. Your consciousness is the focal point for your senses; your thoughts, feelings, and spiritual awareness. From this your free will creates your attitude. It decides your priorities. This mélange is your life. It's your goals and what you'd pay for them. It's your purpose and the Love God promised would protect you. Your welfare is behind every question you ask and every decision you make. Before you can meet the high ideals of your soul's dream you have to stay alive. How you do that amazes God. That's one of the reasons God loves you so much. God knows it's hard to stay alive. Without sustenance, your life ends. But

Creation needs your energy. Every experience has a metaphysical element. Metaphysical simply means it serves God's consciousness.

To stay alive, first you have to breathe. And eat. And drink. You need good hygiene. You need a safe place to sleep. You need a respectful attitude to your relationships, including your environment. You need Love. When you have everything you need then you can explore your existence. Satisfying your needs is your purpose. Every day you work at it. Forget the peace in your prayers as you sort through life's mysteries. Forget the freedom in your creativity that lets you imagine a better world. Forget your free will that constantly questions right and wrong. First you have to respect your physical existence. You need the courage of your self-respect to sustain you. Then you can be an equal partner with God. Together, nothing can stop you; not in life or anywhere else in Creation.

What's this strange thing we call *life*? It's strange because it co-exists with its opposites; both a conscious mind seemingly without form and a physical body that thinks it runs everything. And what's this soul thing about? Life does well when it's nourished. You're whole with the world and you rely on it. Its freshness becomes your freshness. When you're nourished, you do well. It's not easy because what you want may not be available. So, like Nature, you search for it. You're not alone. Everything's dependent. The beauty of dependence is it expands Creation's opportunities by creating more relationships. It puts things together in new ways so it can do more. That's the challenge of human survival; finding connections that support your existence even when they don't yet exist. If you can't, you adapt to your environment till it's unsustainable and you die.

Creatively, you're superior to Nature. You're subject to it, but you enjoy the miracle in God's creativity that lets you remake it. You have to. That's how you get by; that and your body's wonderful design that gives you the ability to do it. Nature finds sustenance where it can while you can buy food at the supermarket from some farmer who grew it on the other side of the world. Instead of getting water from a hygienically unsafe stream, you can enjoy clean water from your kitchen tap. Nature's design keeps you alive. Your design finds ways to make it better. You have imagination. All you want is comfort. Fortunately, you create it. It's your peace. It's your self-respect, confidence, and faith. It's everything you need.

SELF-RESPECT: THE SOLUTION TO UNSOLVABLE PROBLEMS

Your attitude depends on where you are in relation to your goals. It's how you weigh the balance. When you respect it, you know what to expect. Everyone has their own way of doing things. Your success depends on a compromise. It knows your soul's worth isn't the greed society is selling you; popularity, power, and wealth. Still, it's society's best answer. Your task is to create the right balance between survival and your Love for Creation. While you do your best to stay alive, your soul keeps juggling it. So you have to be alert. You don't want to drop it. Shifting balances force you to adjust to what's important at the moment. You have to see how things go together to create opportunities. You want to make a difference, so you have to understand the consequences. You create scenarios for success and try to avoid mistakes. That's what you're up against in this frightening world. Then the question becomes, "How can you control Creation's energy when it has a will of its own?"

You exist in a mix of experience. You learn from everything and throw it in the pot. Depending on how you stir the pot, some parts cook better than others. Some parts rise to the top and others fall to the bottom. You add different flavors in the way of relationships and activities. It all feeds your consciousness. You add some more and develop an attitude toward life. Now it feeds your soul. You taste it. What could make it better? Is it a divine pleasure or just something to eat? Do you feel like you ate too much or do you want more? You know when it makes you uncomfortable. It's an inconvenience but you take care of it and you feel better. The measure of maturity is how you take care of yourself. History weighs your choices, so respect every experience. They become part of you. You'd hate to suffer a problem you could have avoided had you just remembered you've been there before.

Respect your body. How do you do that? The media popularizes food, but you really don't know what it does to you. It answers your hunger but what else? You usually don't ask till you're sick from it. Food diseases are common. Every day you see ads for drugs to combat diabetes or heart disease. You know what eating too much or too little does to your appearance, but what about your survival? You hear about the benefits of exercise and drinking water, but it seems like work. It seems like a sacrifice. It's boring. It doesn't seem necessary. Anyway, food tastes good and you like it. Time decides if you beat a disease or if it beats you. You control your health, from regular check-ups to the vitamins you take. You decide your priorities. You can be the envy of your friends or tragic office gossip. You don't need a trendy regimen, but your body needs attention however you do it. You have to protect your body if you want to trust it.

Your first responsibility is your health. All your opportunities depend on it. You have to love it. Your body makes your imagination real. Most important, it's yours. It gives your soul life. It's your physical presence. It connects your consciousness to the world. You have to respect it; feed it, exercise it, rest it, and challenge it with the utmost care. You have to love everything about it. It relies on you to take care of it. It's durable, but it's fragile. It's the most important thing you have because within it are all your dreams.

You're aware of your health, because you're close to it. Its sensitivities are practical. It fills your consciousness with tactile reactions to life. You physically feel the pleasure and pain. They're signals. Your engagement with life depends on your body's success. Beyond your physical senses, your body senses its well-being. When you're right about your being you're whole with Creation. It's your metaphysical stability. Your psychological health depends on your physical well-being. It's all connected. An irritating thought can become a rash. Hate can become cancer. It's cause and effect, and it doesn't have to be real. It only matters that you believe it. Your beliefs control your body. Are you eating for health or for comfort? I like what Steve Jobs said, "Eat your food like medicine or you'll eat your medicine for food." Know what you're eating. Read the labels. Educate yourself. The wrong food can throw your whole body out of balance. It's not a diet forced on you by your environment, like having to eat whale blubber in the Arctic. Self-respect is the food environment you choose. You don't need a college degree in nutrition. You just have to love your life.

This isn't once and done. Your health is with you every day. It's the balance you constantly recalculate to live the life you want. You have to respect it. It can motivate you or be a burden. It's as inconsequential as a sneeze or life-changing like multiple sclerosis. It's a system. Like your car, you have to maintain every part every day, not just when it's broken. You don't want to be deprived of your car and you don't want to be deprived of your health. It's

SELF-RESPECT: THE SOLUTION TO UNSOLVABLE PROBLEMS

your freedom. It's precious, but you can't buy it no matter how much money you have. You can only negotiate with the promise of self-respect.

Good health is a good routine. It's dependable and flexible. But what if you get sick? Then you have to accommodate it. Health awareness is more than food pyramids and gym class. It's your spiritual attitude toward your body. It's overcoming the inertia of ignoring your health when you feel good. Most of your health is unseen. You accept the challenge of putting gas in your car and getting to work on time. It's how you pay the bills. It's an obvious responsibility, but how do you know when your arteries are building blockages on their way to putting you in the hospital with a heart attack? How do you know when there's too much sugar in your blood setting you up for blindness or death from diabetes? You do it by loving yourself and respecting your health. You get regular check-ups. You get your blood tested. It usually doesn't get real until it's a problem. Then your self-respect protects you by *insisting* you use your common sense and take action...that or you get worse.

But you feel pretty good except for a few small pains. You exercise. You eat right. You look good in the mirror. In your mind you're still twenty-one. So you keep going till something breaks. If there's a problem; you fix it. Human nature naturally breaks down; from a splinter under your fingernail to a bad case of flu. The question becomes, "How do you respect your health when everything seems okay?" Your self-respect moves quickly when you're suffering. Your body warns you before it's out of control. There are signs. There are symptoms. You hurt. You swell. You change color. Or something stops working.

Health is a balance. Fortunately, the cost is small compared to the benefit. You don't want to die from some infection you could have cured with antibiotics from the local pharmacy. Most diseases are manageable. There are support groups where you can learn from other people's experiences so you don't repeat their suffering. You can take precautions like professional athletes who can't afford an injury and risk ruining their livelihood. The money is big and careers are short. So they protect themselves with braces and tape and have ambulances and doctors on the sidelines. You have to know what could happen to your body so you can protect it. Your body has a will of its own. Respect it, because if you don't it will. It knows how to get your attention with some malady. Your health shouldn't be an afterthought neither should it be an obsession. Balance your freedom. You have to decide what's important to you then measure the risk you can tolerate.

Respecting yourself means respecting your body. Your body is independent but you direct it. It's designed to work for you. You resolve the conflict between your soul's sensibilities and your body's demands as part of life. It takes a lot of sweat to work in the field all day. When you love the city, breathing the dirty air seems a small accommodation. You have to find a balance that makes it a worthwhile experience. You need exercise or your muscles will atrophy and weaken. You need fresh air away from the city's noxious fumes to energize you. You need rest. You need sleep. You need to enjoy yourself. You need to restore yourself. You need to find peace with yourself. Excuses don't fool anyone. You're doing this for yourself. You have to take the time you need. Support it and your body will help you as much as it can.

Bad habits and advertising are the challenge, especially if you're confused about nutrition. You don't have to be an expert. You have to respect yourself. Food is compelling even if you aren't hungry. Your body will do anything to stay alive so it needs constant vigilance. The truth is; you're always hungry. You can't be sure where your next meal is coming from and your body depends on it. But you have to know what's good for you. The food industry sells you salt and sugar then the drug companies sell you ways to avoid the effects of salt and sugar. It's confusing. On one side is your pleasure eating delicious foods and on the other side are the illnesses you create by eating foods that burden your body. Self-respect is a coalition of your mind and body telling your body when you've had enough, not your ability to eat another slice of pizza. Protect your limits. Find the balance that respects your body. Good health isn't just a flat belly. It's your body performing at its best with all its elements working together. Love it and trust it. 90% of feeling good is caring about yourself.

Reticence isn't a goal. It's not having a goal. It's hiding from life. It's the choice to be ignorant. You avoid caring but you also miss the Love in caring. You make a doubt bigger than Love when you make it a priority. Engaging life is your strength. You can always do something. You can always learn how. Knowledge gives you the ability. Experience gives you the confidence. The

SELF-RESPECT: THE SOLUTION TO UNSOLVABLE PROBLEMS

message of food is to "be energized." Just because it has flavor doesn't mean that it's food. How many jelly beans can you eat? Food is nutrition. Food gives you strength. Most people don't know what to do with their strength so they hide from it. They hold back to make it easier to control. Self-respect teaches you to embrace your strength. Your soul's role can't be avoided. You're partners with God. Faith is your spiritual strength. Health is your physical strength.

Health defines your ability. Are you full of energy or do you suffer a disease? Each is a different challenge. Your soul is the referee. There's a permanent contest between your soul, your mind, and your body. Like the child who eats too much candy, feasting makes you feel good. But there's often a hangover to remind you, you had a choice. But your soul may accept a terrible disease just for the challenge, something you'd never do if you were making a conscious decision. Is a terrible disease worth the eternal benefit? It takes courage but many people do it. It's a lesson that can't be learned any other way. Your soul knows this. Your mind and body are less agreeable. They want common sense. Your physical needs must be respected. A short-lived pleasure can be a long-term expense. That extra slice of pizza means another 400 calories you have to burn off. A thrilling risk may end in a serious injury. Life is your soul's plan. It could be as trivial as deciding what you want on your taco, or as critical as choosing the daily care you'll need for the rest of your life. That's why you shouldn't judge yourself. Your soul knows there's a good reason for everything, but you often need faith to sustain it.

You need a positive attitude toward your health. If you programmed yourself to think junk food is your happiness then reprogram yourself to eat what's good for you. You can still enjoy it. Modern life is your way past survival. We do pretty well for ourselves. You don't have to risk your health with foods that can harm you. You can laugh away a heart attack or listen to what it's telling you. You're not going to stare it down. You have to choose sides; the potential for life and meeting your responsibilities or the potential for death and the responsibilities you'll leave for someone else. There's nothing to feel deprived about. You simply have to update your habits. No one forces you to eat cake. Advertising does its best to make it attractive so you buy it, but it's your decision. Make it a conscious choice. Surrendering to an old habit is a mistake because you don't have to. You can change it. Whatever you want, you have to do something about it. It takes time to reach your goals. Self-respect is your choice to take the time you need.

Society is always selling you something. First it's eat whatever you like, then it's pills and programs to control your weight and the problems that come from eating the wrong things. The wrong thing will make you feel uncomfortable. It can happen after a party when you feel bloated and hung over or in twenty years when you need open-heart surgery to save your life. But bad things don't have to happen. Your creativity empowers you to change it. You know how to respect your health. It's a little different for each of us. We all like different things, but no justification excuses your responsibility to respect your body. Your attitude toward food is in your mind. It's human nature to overeat. But the odds are you're pretty well-fed now. Then food becomes a game; cooking shows, restaurants, and binging on chocolate. Eating becomes recreation. You just have to convince your body that it's good for you.

The answer to life seems to be to do whatever you want. Just do more of it, often until you're drunk and offensive or trying on a bigger size. Too much of a good thing is a bad thing. That's what "too much" means. Too much risk becomes an accident. Too much food becomes forty pounds overweight. Your body won't accommodate "too much" of anything; not too much salt, too much sugar, or too much alcohol. It's your responsibility to measure it. Problems can get worse. It's not the pain of nicking yourself shaving. You can pull away from that pain. Ignoring your health is a slow descent until you crash. It's a cavity becoming a root canal. It's ignoring a sunburn while your skin turns red. You know it's happening but will you prioritize it enough to get out of the sun? Is your search for the perfect tan so important that you'd risk letting your skin burn? And could your decision to accept the damage burden you with a bigger problem later?

If you think a problem is unsolvable it's because you haven't done enough to solve it. You haven't used enough pressure to loosen the cap. You haven't been patient enough to accept the timing. Life is more than a 30 second traffic light. It'll take as long as it takes. You have to respect yourself and believe you can do it. You have to open your mind to your opportunities even if you first have to create them. The result doesn't matter. It's the quest. The answers are everywhere. Don't let social norms interfere with you being fair

SELF-RESPECT: THE SOLUTION TO UNSOLVABLE PROBLEMS

to yourself. When it comes to anything about you, you're the answer. You're the one who decides a fair balance. You're the one who suffers when you're out of balance. Your body shows you how you're doing through your health. Its simple message is comfort or pain. So pay attention and don't worry about it. The answer always comes.

Self-respect is your attention to yourself. It knows what you need. It knows what you want. It's having the courage to give yourself what you want. Self-awareness is more than your body. You have to look into your consciousness and ask yourself, "Are your soul's questions being answered? Is your work on yourself going the way you had hoped?" Then ask yourself, "Are your life's questions being answered? Do you like what you're doing every day? Are you on your way to having what you want?" Your path begins with your goals and an honest assessment of where you are. You're not achieving anything without a goal. You'll wind up somewhere, but likely wherever the wind blows you. Creative freedom gives you the ability to characterize your goals with the features you like. Then, as you grow, you learn the details are just as important as the plan.

Your goals define you. They tell you where you are, where you want to be, and how you can get there. They're the same paths walked by billions of people before you. You're ready for your adventure. It's not going to be all sunny days but it's the adventure you chose. Good times and bad both need attention and they all have things to teach you. Whatever you do, you're trying to make your life better. That's what you're doing now. That's what you're always doing. It's the wisdom of comparing success and failure in Rudyard Kipling's poem "*If.*" "And treat both those imposters the same." Life is your adventure, every part of it. Society trusts success is having the most. People get so weird that they brag who has the worst disease. Anything, as long as it's the most. Life's tragedies are entertaining as long as they're not happening to you…and sometimes even when they happen to you. "Do you want to sign my cast?" Life may not always be fun but it's always interesting.

Your first sense is to "survive." Is the air fit to breathe? Is the water safe to drink? Are the plants and animals edible? When the answer is "no" it can kill you. Before you spend your day praying with the guru you have to survive. It's a spiritual mandate. It directs everything you do. It's the same as a newborn gasping for its first breath. Your body needs oxygen for your soul to stay connected. Breathing is life. Some people breathe better in the mountains. Some like a balmy ocean breeze. Peace starts with trusting your breath. Each breath fulfills the promise of survival. It's the bridge between life and death. It's your courage and faith. A labored breath is fearful. A relaxed breath is at peace.

Be alert. When a lion jumps out at you there's an obvious danger. You remove the danger or you'll be eaten. But threats don't always jump out at you. They creep up like a python and wrap around you till there's no chance of escape and squeeze the life out of you. That's how a problem outmaneuvers you. They present themselves subtly and even though you brush them away they can linger. Then they grow. That's why your attention is important. You have to keep questioning your environment and make sure it's not a problem…or an opportunity if you have a positive attitude. Identify the situation and you're ready to handle it.

Whatever you think, peace is in your self-respect. Appreciate it. Live by it. It connects you to God's respect for you as an individual. Self-respect is your mind's connection to God. Know it. Believe it. Survival is about awareness. That's why it's called consciousness. It's situational awareness with a universal focus. You have to see yourself as part of Creation. When you trust you have a place here, you can make the adjustments that give you what you want. Self-respect gauges everything. The success of your self-respect is in loving yourself. It's your faith in God and belief in yourself. It trusts Love's support and enjoys being part of it.

Nature supports your survival. It's an important part in God's plan. Like a deer running from a forest fire, it wants you to survive. You live with situations that aren't perfect but they support you. The conundrum is your soul's not concerned about survival. Its world is Eternity and it'll use any experience to learn more about it. There's a long line waiting to be born as a conjoined twin. There aren't that many opportunities. Your soul has a unique nature. It works with life's energies. Organizing Nature is your job. Your creativity makes it a never-ending question. But how do you cooperate with it when it can kill you? Where's the compromise in that? Competition wants a direction because winning defines it. But it should be a loving experience like every other experience you have. That's why businesses have trade associations even though they compete in the same industry. Cooperation is

SELF-RESPECT: THE SOLUTION TO UNSOLVABLE PROBLEMS

the answer, whether it's forming a new solar system or deciding what to do on a date. With Love, Nature emulates God's unity for a purpose greater than itself.

Some people can't survive by themselves. Their self-respect is their appreciation for what others can do for them. Their self-respect comes from doing their best as limited as it is. You can't negotiate with a wheel chair. If you need it, you need it. Self-respect isn't being the lone wolf. It sees an opportunity in working together. Even then, it's risky. You want to be fair but you don't want to sacrifice your values. Your values are your self-respect. Unfairness festers as a hidden hatred and must be resolved. A self-respecting person won't accept unfairness. It's the antithesis of self-respect. You control fairness by demanding it. Without fairness, impatience becomes anger. Disappointment becomes self-pity. And your fears become irrational. The bottom line is you feel bad. Life's a negotiation and you can only control your side of it. Hope for a fair agreement. Life's too much to do by yourself.

Whatever compromise you make, it has to honor your self-respect. It's where your Peace survives. It's your trust in yourself. Self-respect expresses spiritual values. It's the goodness you want for yourself. Whether you find it through a political movement or a friend at work, you need good advice. You need a healthy attitude. You need a proper balance. You want to respect the path you're on. You want to respect your purpose. You want your life to have meaning. "Meaning" is a positive point of view. It might be to have a successful business or be a scientist and make amazing discoveries. It could be a life of service or fulfilling your role as a leader. Everything's okay. You just have to realize that to be successful Love must be part of it. Love gives your life meaning. You have to love every part of yourself, especially the parts you want to improve. You have to care about yourself and respect God's role in it. There's always a connection. You just have to find it.

Competition is life's motive. Even when you're asleep, you have to breathe. And with every breath you challenge death. Will you enjoy another day of life or will your body return to the earthly world it came from? Life means opportunities. You want your life to be better, so you question it. You innovate. God wants you to use your opportunities and be confident. When you're confident your courage will lead you through life's mysteries. "Why am I here?" is a great question. But once you get past the details there's not much left; just nuances on nuances. When you see Love is the basis for everything, you've found your peace regardless of the circumstances. When you have what you need, you're happy. When you're missing something, you're unhappy. Everything fits that logic…until you add Love. With Love everything succeeds. Love helps the needy and helps those blessed with abundance too. Everyone needs something or they wouldn't be here. Understanding that should keep you busy the rest of your life.

The question becomes, "Where's your responsibility?" How can we stop pollution and still enjoy the benefits of manufacturing? How do we help a subsistence culture enjoy the benefits of technology without destroying their way of life? Solving those problems is a necessity but not a priority. Your attitude is the priority. Your children's welfare is your first concern. Raising the standard of living *for everyone* is the work of civilization. Survival is God's challenge. No matter what, you'll always be a success in God's eyes. God knows life is hard. God knows you make mistakes. So respect yourself, be sincere, and accept God's Love. You're part of Creation so God helps you. God knows you'll overcome your problems because only God matters when it comes to keeping score. It's what God learns from your experience that makes your life worthwhile. It's impossible to fail. Your experience is the achievement.

Success and failure are human concepts. Your mandate is to stay alive. Your soul's mandate is to create more Love. To sacrifice your life for Love is the most challenging choice you can make. It could mean working a second job to make enough money to send your kid to college. It could mean entering a frozen lake to rescue a stranger stuck on the ice. Or it could mean joining the military to defend your way of life. You have to decide if it's worth the trouble. It's never easy when life or death is your choice. In the end, your self-respect must be satisfied when your values are weighed. The first question is, "Can you succeed?" You don't really know. You won't know till you try. A life or death test is rare, thank God. Most problems give you time to think. Running to a burning car to pull someone out won't give you much time to think. All you can do is pray you make the right decision and hope you survive. Whatever happens, respect yourself because you'll live with those judgments the rest of your life. You can forgive yourself if you're honest. Honesty is your self-respect. Common sense isn't always an easy answer.

SELF-RESPECT: THE SOLUTION TO UNSOLVABLE PROBLEMS

As soon as you're born you're confronted by your needs. Life is needs; physical, psychological, and spiritual needs. Comfort is your guide. Comfort is your self-respect. Your physical presence has questions and your spiritual presence answers them. Love creates the balance. Love is God's awareness of itself. Your job is to balance life's mish-mash and create loving experiences. It's a fun game when you get it right. But it's stressful when you're sick, you can't pay your bills, or social conflicts won't leave you alone. You get frustrated because you don't know how to fix them. That's the game. That's why you need faith. Fears can blind you. Disappointments may be irrational. Everything eventually ends and you start again. With a positive outlook, life's fascinating. That's why you laugh at old hurts. You realize your maturity can't be forced. Your self-respect knows it takes time. All you can do is coax good fortune the best you can.

Survival can be a heartfelt hope or a nagging fear. It's your choice. You decide when you reached your goal. You decide if you're aligned with your values. You do whatever helps. You try to understand the possibilities; the dangers and opportunities. So you have to pay attention. You have to respect the uncertainty in the turn of each card. Life is miserable when you're losing, fun when you're winning, and it only ends when you die. But as long as you're playing, you can aim for a better life.

Chapter 5
Your Success Is In You.

The question is, "How can you be successful?" It doesn't matter how you define it. It only matters that you succeed. Goals evolve. Even when you're successful you want more. You want what's bad to be good and what's good to be better. Respect your imagination. You have to characterize your dream. You need faith. You have to trust yourself because within you is the answer. You know what you like. It's usually the first thing that comes to mind. Trust yourself even when it challenges what you think you know. Ask yourself, "Where's your happiness?" There's an inclination to compare yourself to social values instead of appreciating the possibilities in your creativity. The world is always looking for new ideas, especially with computers doing the work. When a new idea is your first response, it's worth considering.

You may think you don't know, but you do. You just need to tighten the connection between your subconscious mind and your daily consciousness. Whether it's through meditation or contemplating philosophies, it's all in your head. That's where your dreams are. That's where your soul connects to God's consciousness. They're beliefs centered on Love. It may just be a feeling, but you know you like it. It's intriguing. You just don't want to waste your time striving for someone else's goal. You want your responsibility on your own terms. It means expressing yourself for who you are. It means respecting the creative wisdom God gave you. It's hard separating your thoughts from what the world thinks you should think. There's good sense in civilization, but it shouldn't limit you. With a little thought you can have it all. Everything's processed through your values, but they often speak in low tones so you have to listen closely.

You have to be brave even when it takes you in a new direction. You have to make choices but you're good at making choices. It's the original question,

"What do you want?" It might be to be an actor or jump off a mountain on a hang glider. You could be a truck driver or a scientist. You could be a leader, a follower, or mind your own business. It's hard to believe you have a choice because it takes a commitment. The more complex it is, the more you have to learn. You don't see a lot of ten year old doctors, but come back in thirty years and that kid on the playground might be putting a new heart in your chest. So respect potential. Maturity takes time. You can't force it. You have to work with it. That means patience. God's grace aligns your life with the Universe. No one can take it from you. But it takes its own time.

Ask good questions. You'll know the answer when you see it. It'll make sense to you. You know what you're looking for. You know what you like...and what you don't like. Your sincerity reveals it. The challenge is to know what's right for you...and your willingness to pay for it. There are social rules. There are the laws of physics. You're part of the mass consciousness and it's part of you. Whatever influences you, you have to accept it even when it adds responsibilities. Accept the reality that serves a good purpose. Society is people working to get along with each other. It's not magic. It's people doing their best to share a common experience. Each of us contributes to society so society can do a better job taking care of us. Every society wants to improve itself. It's a balancing act because the rules we agree on affect everyone differently.

Peace is your satisfaction. Peace is your comfort with God. Self-respect judges your values. You have a responsibility to decide what right and wrong mean to you. Your free will defines it. Self-respect is your satisfaction with the process. Whatever you want comes from Nature. Socially, it's a venue somebody else provides like a job or a goodnight kiss. Confidence comes from knowing what you want. The praise that honors your confidence will come from someone else. Recognition matters. It supports your belief that you were right to commit to your values. It's your reward. It proves you're a winner, not just in your eyes but in a world where everyone competes for everything.

People often see money as a trophy. It's the universal symbol of success. It's ownership and power. It can give you an enviable life. But it's not necessary to an enviable life. Your happiness is the greatest possession you can have and you give it to yourself. Real success is having what you want. It's more

SELF-RESPECT: THE SOLUTION TO UNSOLVABLE PROBLEMS

than ownership. It's more than getting it any way you can. It's respecting your values in the way you get it. It's how you love everyone in this pressure cooker of competition. It's where you draw the line between your success and someone else's failure. Competition has winners and losers. But there are degrees of success. It doesn't have to be all or nothing. Participating in a marathon is a success. Completing a marathon is a greater success. Finishing in the top ten is a rare success. And winning is the ultimate success reserved for but a few.

The question with success is, "What do you do once you have everything?" Is your peace only in the rising numbers of your bank account? When you judge yourself, do you compare yourself to who has the most money? Is your joy a bank statement full of numbers or using that money to take your dream vacation? Passive investment isn't action. Action is involvement. Action is being part of the business, doing the work, and creating your reward. Life is about taking risks. It's the fulfillment of Love's challenge to be successful; to question life, care about it, and care about others. It's more than Super Bowl tickets or eating in a fancy restaurant. It's your understanding that your opportunities never end. It knows that your responsibilities should equal your abilities.

Money is reassuring. You have bills to pay and there are always taxes and insurance coming up. So how should you spend your riches? Contributing to something everyone can use, like a library, is a good way to love your community. Donating to an organization that delivers services to the homeless is a compassionate thing to do. But service isn't a number. It's a moral value. It's a mindset. Its success depends on your sincerity. Money can't solve every problem. And more money doesn't do any better. Ideas solve problems. You're competing against Nature. Your health can't be forced no matter how much money you have. Your sincerity attracts Nature's healing. It's your Love for Creation. It sees Creation as your partner. Creation balances on Love. Love connects everything. It's your health, wealth, and self-respect.

You need help. It's a big step from where you are to where you want to be. So you have to invest in yourself. You do it through Creation. Creation lets you work with everything. You have to connect the parts that match your dream. The good news is there are unlimited ways to do it. Your enthusiasm keeps it together. Your money creates the resources. And your resources create the opportunities. Spending money is easy. Income is the challenge because it depends on other people. They have to believe that giving you their money is in their best interests. That's how you make money. You get it from your customers, investors, and supporters. You get it from people who believe in you. A customer expects something useful in return. An investor expects more money. And a supporter expects you to succeed. For them, money is just another way of loving you.

You trade what you have to get what you want, but it's always an expression of Love. It could be the bank giving you a loan so you can buy a house and build equity as a homeowner. It could be the customer who eats at your restaurant every day that insures your business success. Love is also the way you make money. It's a good education or a talent you can offer. Eventually you find the right formula and keep it going as long as you can. But what's your motivation when you have enough money for a thousand lifetimes? What are you creating then that's worth your time? Is it a school for the under-privileged or another night of overpriced debauchery? Wealth is a fantastic opportunity for the dreamer but a problem if you're selfish. Nature is innately productive. That's your responsibility. You're its engine. Nature lives in the future. Its dream is to grow. Selfishness lives in the past and aimlessly chases more selfishness.

You have assets. You have God's Love and the Universe's support. You have free will. You have Creation waiting for your command. You have enthusiasm, the Love that defines Creation's ambition. Love empowers everything and it believes in you 100%. Your soul wants you to succeed. You give life a vision. Love what you dream about. Don't make intransigent demands. Allow Creation to help you. God wants you to question everything. You can define happiness any way you like but it needs a definition. It needs a purpose. That's up to you. It shouldn't just mean more money. That's the lazy way out no matter how hard you work for it. It's an excuse for not using your creativity. Your imagination gives you limitless possibilities. Don't let possessions be your happiness. Joy is your happiness and it doesn't cost you anything. It's in your attitude. You have to be happy with who you are. You have to respect yourself and know you're doing your best.

SELF-RESPECT: THE SOLUTION TO UNSOLVABLE PROBLEMS

You don't have to sacrifice your self-respect to accommodate a problem. Still, you may have to compromise to get along with a boorish in-law. It's a value judgement. One time a year at Thanksgiving isn't the best time to make demands. Then how far should you go for peace in your family? How much can you limit your self-respect and still be at peace with yourself? Self-respect measures how you balance your values. It's the Peace in your peace of mind. It may be uncomfortable but as long as you want balance, you can survive creepy in-laws with your self-respect intact. Compromise is the answer to social problems. If that doesn't work, it's time to move on. The more important issue is how you deal with being disrespected.

Self-aggrandizement is a contrivance for limiting emotional pain. You fool yourself into an illusion of superiority. You create resentments that target someone else as the villain instead of accepting your own responsibility. It's your self-respect trying to explain why life doesn't treat you better. You justify who you are in an environment where people don't care because they're busy juggling their own lives. Your sincerity supports an honest picture of yourself. But when you add life's burdens it can be a bear to handle. Life moves fast, then it slows down to a crawl. There's too much, then there's barely anything. That's Nature. Self-respect is the way you adapt. Where maturity is your goal, every experience is an opportunity. You may want comfort, but engaging life is the way you achieve it. It's keeping pace with the changing balance between your needs and responsibilities. Failure explains how hard it is to make the right connection every time. God is always there when you need it. You may lose your life, but there's always another day.

See the silver lining. The old adage is true. The answer may lie hidden under layers of rationalizations. Problems create opportunities you wouldn't have without them. Usually, you do your best to avoid a problem. As a child you learned to look both ways before you crossed the street. Then you matured to the challenge of your ambitions and learned to create opportunities. You found better ways to use your time than just worrying about things. No matter what your situation, your self-respect helps you. It only ends when you give up. That's what *"Your success is in you."* means. Nature's resistance is the same for everyone. Ask yourself, "What works best for you?" Is it your dedication or doing the least you can to survive? How can you trust something if it takes so long? Do you have the patience to let it develop?

That's maturity. All you can do is push on it till it yields...or sends you in a new direction. Life is how you manage it. It's how you manage yourself.

What's success worth to you? What would you sacrifice for it? It might drop into your lap; winning the lottery or being born with an amazing talent. But if you're like the other seven billion people here on Earth you probably have to make a plan and work at it. Success is work. It's your choice to invest yourself in it. You can enjoy the process when you respect yourself. The end isn't having the job you want. It's being happy with the job you want. Maybe the job lives up to your expectations and maybe it doesn't. There are many young attorneys who can't hack the grind of fighting in court. So restart the process and find something better. It could be just an aspect of the system they don't like. With experience they can focus on the parts they do like. The aspiration to be happy is everyone's goal. Make the compromises you must but try to do better. As long as your goal exists; you can reach it.

Relationships are important to your consciousness. You can feel the Love in everyone. It's life. It's existence. Life should be interesting, not just another margarita to kill the day. You can do whatever you like...so do it. Feel the wonder in life. Name it. Is it traveling the world to experience new cultures or anticipating the fun in a game of tennis? You have options. That's the fun of it. But you have to make the effort. It takes courage to be successful because you don't know if you'll like it till you try. No one's asking you to walk to the North Pole, but you have to be brave enough to challenge your doubts. If you're worried what others might think, know you're a passing thought to them unless they love you like family. They have their own problems. You're a minute's diversion; not that important and easily forgotten...unless you're successful. Then you'll have their attention because they want to be successful too. They want to know how you did it. You can change your plan but hold onto your dream. And don't worry. You have plenty of time.

You have to feel your life is worth caring about. It's valuable. Self-respect means you value yourself for who you are. It measures your demands on yourself. It can be hard when you drive yourself hell-bent on success or peaceful as you concede to a child who wants to touch your face. Think how you compromise your self-respect when you ride the crowded bus to work every day. You control your self-respect by being conscious of it. To others you may mean nothing unless you make it clear you expect to be respected.

SELF-RESPECT: THE SOLUTION TO UNSOLVABLE PROBLEMS

You don't have to carry a sword wherever you go. You don't have to sneer your disdain when you feel your self-respect is challenged. Stand your ground with a loving heart. Confidence comes from believing in yourself despite the circumstances. Peace asks you to tolerate the human condition. When you accept reasonable compromises, reasonable people will respect you.

Self-respect is the key. If you don't respect yourself you'll have to depend on the world's generosity. People look out for themselves. If you show weakness, expect to be exploited. Compromise isn't weakness. It's cooperation based on everyone's needs and understanding you can do more when you work together. Every relationship balances on respect. Will your boss respect you for working late? Will you respect the clerk who gave you too much change? A boss will show their appreciation by paying you more. You respect the clerk by correcting the error and returning the overage. Respect is Love's balance. If you want more then give more and add more Love in the bargain.

If there's a better balance, you'll find it. Ideas are designed for balance. When you respect yourself you respect your ideas. When you approach a problem with a purpose, there's always one idea that supports the others...the solution. Get help when you need it. Help is the beauty of civilization. It's more than an extra back to carry the load. It's the increase in ideas that find a better way to carry the load. You don't have physical problems. You have idea problems. The first question is, "Is solving this problem necessary?" The solution may be to ignore it. Compare your options. You don't want to take a shortcut that winds up taking you longer. In your rush to get to work you don't want to get stopped for speeding. Then the time you gained is wasted fixing the problem you created. Your goal isn't fixing problems. Your goal is your happiness. Love doesn't rush. It finds better ways of doing things.

Relationships are a challenge. Like a car's suspension balancing the weight to create a smoother ride, they're a level of awareness that seeks harmony in different experiences. Support underlies healthy relationships. Old friends. Young lovers. National pride. Any way people associate, there's a measure of creativity to explore it. It's not generic. It has your name on it. Relationships are your interest in Creation. Your success depends on the way you frame it; how you respect it. You can make it anything you want. But you don't live in a vacuum. Everything's connected. You may not need the adoration of a million fans. Maybe one good friend is all you can handle. Find Paradise where you can... then love it with all your might.

It doesn't take effort. It takes courage. So you move from the suburbs to the city, then from Long Island to Florida. Every place has a story and a different way of doing things. Even when you accept the responsibility, you still need relationships. At least you need the trust of some good friends. When you pray to the Universe, you always get an answer. The hard part is when the Universe tells you to wait. You may not like it but it's a sincere reaction...and an education. The solution is creating relationships with the right people; tolerant people who love you for who you are. People want to trust you. Trust is safe. Trust is patient. Trust is caring. And caring supports you.

Your success depends on others. Whatever success means to you, it'll likely come from someone else. You can toil at your easel and make beautiful paintings, but if you aren't recognized who'll buy them and how will you pay for your paints? A pat on the back is good. A kind word or constructive criticism is encouraging. Everyone needs encouragement. Life's a grind. Success is a mixture of hard work and destiny. Destiny doesn't change so you have to do your best with what you have. Some things you control and some things you can't. A terrible mistake won't sink your destiny and there's no way to speed it up either. It has a purpose in its schedule. It needs the pieces to fit together in a certain way to create the right opportunities. And it can turn on a dime. Your destiny can pull you up or drag you down so it's important to have a positive attitude about it. It's ordained by God and agreed to by you. Go with it. It makes you a positive force in the Universe. Your Peace is in your acceptance of it. What you do with it is up to you.

Success is your destiny. You can't avoid a problem if it's your destiny. You wouldn't want to. It's something you have to do. Your destiny is the plan you and God worked out for your life. Your humanity wants life's benefits but your soul wants the challenges. Your soul can handle it. Life isn't designed to defeat you. Love protects you. You're born with creativity and common sense but you decide your attitude. Your success must respect your feelings. Every decision you make should feel good. That's what a positive attitude means. It's hard because different choices have different responsibilities. Trust your desire to do well. Success is magical. It shouts, "Hang in there! Don't defeat yourself! Good things are coming!" Make the decision to be a positive

SELF-RESPECT: THE SOLUTION TO UNSOLVABLE PROBLEMS

person. Have hope. Hope is the belief that Love will get you what you want. You can have terrible problems but the hardship is diminished when you believe you'll get through them. Then you can enjoy your destiny however it comes.

You control your destiny...to a degree. You can't avoid it. Certainty is the meaning of destiny. You can accommodate it though. You can learn to live with it. Life's easier when you accept it. Acceptance forces you to evaluate your expectations in the light of reality. It opens the door to your self-respect so you can stop suffering. It requires patience but you can use that time to train for the success God planned for you. It's a lovely idea to win the lottery and buy all the things you see on TV, but it's the small steps you take each day that give you peace of mind. Wanting something is part of the process. It prepares you for the exquisite feeling when you finally have it. Whatever you want, you want to feel good about it. Feeling good is your goal. Feeling good is how you master fate. Feeling good is your self-respect.

How can you find peace with a destiny you don't like? What if you dream of playing sports but you can't walk? You have two choices. Give up or find a way. You can be a sports announcer or sell memorabilia. You can find somewhere people compete with the same limits. You may not score a hundred points in the NBA but you can share the feeling of victory. You can be the one taking the last shot when time runs out...and scoring! There's always a way to win. You can suffer a problem or do what you can to beat it. Being at peace with your destiny isn't accommodating a failure. It doesn't see failure. It looks for the next positive step. Destiny is your future. Learn from your mistakes. If there's nothing to learn then do something else. Self-respect depends on the positive values you share with your destiny. Eternal values are more important than anything you'll ever do here. Self-respect supports your values. If positive values aren't part of your success, you'll never be happy.

The future is far away. Most problems have no long-term effect. Still, it could be the rest of your life. More likely, it's just another day. It won't be Eternity. Spirit is kinder than that. Trust your destiny. It has your best interests in mind. Life's purpose is to question your destiny. In the good times you have fewer questions. You can enjoy letting your free will wander. There's less urgency to make a change because everything's going well. But that doesn't serve God's purpose. God questions its existence in the way you meet life's challenges. And that usually means too much of something. That's the reality of your partnership with God. Your difficulties, no matter how brutal, are mitigated by the Love you share with Creation. Physical problems end, then Love will show you how your self-respect can blossom.

Free will defines your self-respect. It's not a problem until it's a challenge. When things go well, you're at peace. But things don't always go well and fighting for your values is a common practice. Life's designed like that. The part of you that questions your existence is your connection to God. Its blessing keeps you pulling at the bit racing toward your goal. Free will challenges your humanity. You have to find ways to cooperate with different opinions. Does your spiritual nature guide you or does your human nature compel you? That choice is the way you control your life; holding on, standing up, and getting where you want in one piece. Wild as a bronco or stubborn as a mule, speed doesn't matter. Control is what you need because you can take it wherever you like.

Success is the balance between right and wrong where every shade of gray matters. It's mind control with you as the controller. Every choice you make is a success. Failure is just another part of the experience. You hope you'll be successful but life has a will of its own. Then, what's important? Love is important. Your questions are important. That's for everyone. You, personally? Your survival is important. Your values are important. Your creativity is important. The proof is you exist or Nature would have no need for you. God thinks you're important so you're here. You have Love for yourself, Love for others, and Love for Creation. Love says to respect yourself and care about others. Easy? No way. Life is hard and compromise even harder. Just look at politics. Everyone's agenda doesn't fit. But that's where your happiness is. You may dislike compromising but that's how we all get along. You have to tolerate it. The benefits are worth it. That's why it's important to ask, "Where's the compromise when everyone matters?"

You're really asking, "Where's the balance?" It depends on your interpretation. Self-respect requires that you compare complex values. (A) rarely equals (B). Essentially they may appear alike, but life can give them opportunities in unexpected ways. Decisions are complicated. Different values have different requirements. There are hidden agendas. You can't count on everything you see. You can't count on everything you're told.

SELF-RESPECT: THE SOLUTION TO UNSOLVABLE PROBLEMS

Competing benefits cause the advantage to shift from one option to another. There's a different cost to every consideration. You need to trust the details because it's your responsibility to decide what's fair. You're the only one who knows what your satisfaction feels like.

Every decision you make is a balance between what you want and what you have to do to get it. You may think life is unfair when you see someone with something you want. You feel hurt but it's a waste of time and makes you feel worse. Jealousy is a misguided sense of responsibility. It's your guilt saying you haven't achieved what you want while somebody else has. You can only live your own life. You have to play the cards you're dealt. Comparing yourself to others, unless it's to motivate you, has no useful purpose. Other people's money and other people's things are their responsibility, not yours. Your earthly accomplishments aren't a judgment of who you are as a person. That's what's confusing. Success isn't a lifestyle. It's how you value your choices. Everyone has problems. Everyone has advantages and disadvantages. You do your best. The balance is up to God. Your job is to prioritize your values. Will it be courage or fear? You have to live with the answer so do your best to get it right.

Self-respect is the proof of your maturity. Problems don't end. Once you accomplish your goal, you want to help someone accomplish their goal. Free will is the miracle of creativity. It's the foundation for your maturity. It understands that every soul needs help. Self-respect appreciates life's challenge. It needs that challenge. It's how you build your character. Character is eternal. It survives your life experience. It's your eternal personality. It wins even when you don't like the price. No one likes wearing a cast but that's how bones heal. It's Nature. Your responsibility is to face nature and make better choices. That's the purpose of growing up; to get better at making choices. Your responsibility isn't to succeed at everything. Your responsibility is to engage life, value yourself as an equal, and share the Love in Creation.

Chapter 6
Self-Talk

You spend your whole day talking to yourself. It's a conversation between your conscious and subconscious minds. You think. You consider. You compare. You process where you are, where you want to be, and what you have to do to get there. Your emotions keep telling you how you're doing. You choose your priorities…and what they're worth to you. Your values become your responsibility. Your thoughts justify your values through Love's logic. They support you as the independent soul you are. This keeps the whole process balanced despite all the free will running around. This is Love. This is life. This is your self-respect; how you consider yourself and how you live with it. It's your belief that you can have whatever you want and still respect others. What it means to you specifically, that you have to learn.

How you spend your time reflects your priorities. When you're young you depend on your family to show you how life works. You learn to work with measurements so you can create order and make Nature useful. You study science to see how life interacts with itself. Then you pick something you like and work at it to make a living…if you're lucky. If not, you do what you can to survive. Before you can express your potential as a human being you have to survive. The danger isn't starvation. It's boredom. It's having time you don't know how to use. That's the fantasy in drugs or any substitute for your creativity. They don't accomplish anything. They just waste time. Time becomes eating candy instead of having a good meal. You may fall into the trap of avoidance. You don't know what to do so you don't do anything. Life is work. It's easier to ignore it. Unfortunately, you can't ignore your self-respect because you need it to survive.

You can prize a tasty beer but most people drink to get drunk. They lean on the image in the advertising as much as the taste. It becomes a ceremony.

They love what getting drunk represents as well as the pleasure in being inebriated. It's the same for anything you love. That's why people wear shirts with bright logos. It's a statement of who you are. You probably don't do much else, because there's no reason to make an effort. It's a convenience, not a cause. It's not marching to raise money for the homeless or educating yourself for a new career. You settle into the comfortable avoidance of being a spectator. It's the easiest thing you can do. If you pushed yourself you could be on the company bowling team or volunteer at the library. You congratulate the people who do, but the truth is that person could be you.

Instead of gossiping about some celebrity on TV ask yourself, "How could that person be me?" Justify your self-respect. Admire yourself and be the person you want to be...in your achievements. Bold fantasies and wild cheers only express your desire. You have to do the work. You have to make it happen. It takes effort. It takes time. It takes your commitment; not an argument about who's the best but by being the best.

It's a challenge to know yourself. You have to be honest. You want to be the best you can. An illusion eventually bites you in the ass. Appreciate yourself. Let that be your goal. You don't have to like your situation, but be objective about it. Question yourself. Acknowledge your doubts. Compare your values. Accept your feelings. Are they reasonable? Do they reflect your maturity or are they a knee-jerk reaction to an imagined threat? Have an opinion about everything even if it's trivial. If it exists, it matters to someone. You have to find your place in society. And it's your right to change it. You need an opinion of God and a sense of responsibility. Be cautious with advice but respect loving thoughts. This all swirls around in your head. What would you change? What must you accept? There's a way to be happy, and you're the only one who knows it.

You need a judge you can trust. That's you. That's why self-respect is important to solving your problems. It takes courage. It takes training. Few are born heroes. You have to learn to trust your courage. There's a heroic part of you whether asking for a raise or speaking to a crowd. You stand up for yourself. The scary stuff is rare but the everyday stuff is just as challenging. That's why we admire bravery. You want to be brave too. You want to shield yourself from life's disappointments, but you never can. Life's designed to confront you. That's God's plan. You wouldn't eat chocolate cake every day

SELF-RESPECT: THE SOLUTION TO UNSOLVABLE PROBLEMS

even though it tastes good. Sometimes is fine but every day is too much. It becomes bad for you. You need a comfortable balance between good and bad. Self-respect is that balance. The beauty is self-respect does it without judging you.

Life is problems, so take the good with the bad and don't worry about it. You have to get the job done even when you're desperate. Avoiding desperation is the answer to your problems. You have to think clearly so look at your options. Create more options if you can. How in God's world can you win against a problem designed by God? You do it by understanding what God is trying to do. It's a test where everybody passes. Life can be awful sometimes with poverty, crime, war, and disease. Maybe you survive and maybe you don't. Maybe you suffer and maybe it won't be so bad. To find Peace you have to know what you're living for. Is it another lobster dinner? Is it so good that you'd wait two hours for it? Does a glass of expensive wine impress you? I think it all tastes awful and if it didn't get you drunk no one would drink the stuff, #cocktails. But you're entitled to what you like whether it's old stamps or a closet full of clothes. They give you pleasure. That's fine. But unless you'd give them up without a whimper and be grateful for when you had them you've traded God's Love for a world of ephemeral things. Self-respect opens that door. Then it's your job to reinterpret it and decide what's really worth your time.

Ask yourself for the answer. You know what makes you feel good. You choose your values and decide your priorities. You analyze what you like and why you like it. Are you paid enough? Is it worth your time to be around someone you don't like? You evaluate everything and look for the benefit. You do it consciously *and* subconsciously. Thoughts come to you and you consider them; practical or not, enjoyable or not, and necessary or not. This is self-talk. It's how you consider your life. Your goals surround your self-respect and turn you into an atomic powerhouse. You have free will. So ask yourself, "Is everything happening the way you want? Are your compromises fair? Do you trust what you believe?" And, "What should you do next?"

Think how you were raised and the environments you experienced. Question everything from every point of view. Every time you find an answer you create a new balance. It's your choice to enjoy the situations you like or believe you can make into something you like. The grace is, besides God, you only have to answer to yourself. Accept that responsibility. Don't think you don't know how. You do know or you're meant to learn it. It's your nature to grow through experience. There's always an answer. Be patient. It'll come to you.

Dogma can't do it all. Dogma is an average of beliefs that serves most people but can't do it for everyone. The facts must align with your beliefs. Common sense is a fact. It's the wisdom in your self-respect. Trust your sincerity. You must be willing to change your opinion when the facts support a change. You have to understand that most people don't trust themselves. They'll follow a charismatic leader without even thinking. You can't afford that just because it makes your life easier. You have to think for yourself if you want to be free. You have to question everything. The right thing isn't always the easiest. What's easy today could weigh on you in the future. You wouldn't make a careless decision about your car and not expect to have a problem later. Good decisions are reliable. Don't shy away from your wisdom because it takes work. If that's the only thing bothering you, then get to work. The Universe is a good partner. It's always on your side.

Encourage yourself through affirmations. Train yourself to be a positive person. It could be as simple as telling yourself "You can do this!" on your first day at work. In the same way you train your body to be strong, train your mind not to give up even when you have to change course. You can win on your worst day. You may be physically spent and emotionally exhausted, but you always have the *will* to succeed. Tell yourself you can do it. With all your responsibilities, you decide your purpose. Make it your passion. Focus on it. Don't give thoughts of failure a second chance. Release the energy in negative thoughts. Release the attention that gives them life. Problems aren't failures. Problems are turning points. Change here. Slow down there. In your loving consciousness, do whatever it takes. Your enthusiasm boosts you into hyper drive. Whether you believe it or not, psychic connections help you. You're not alone. Creation embraces you wherever you are and knows you'll do your best.

Maybe you don't win. There are always winners and losers. You might compete against someone with the same skills as you. Life's a riddle and you have to answer it. There's you and God which is a bit of a trick because God is everything. But it's everything from a single point of view, "How will you

SELF-RESPECT: THE SOLUTION TO UNSOLVABLE PROBLEMS

create Love here?" The answer is what you need to succeed. It's inspiring because you know that you're safe. The unknown is fascinating. But when it becomes routine, like a boring job or a tired trend, you need something fresh. Freshness is your unlimited potential. It's exciting. It reveals the unknown. Life doesn't have to be a terrifying ride on a roller coaster. Excitement isn't always danger. Ask an artist who's made the final decision their artwork is finished. Satisfaction is their thrill that, for that moment, they've made sense of the world. And it can be your thrill too for the Love *you* create.

Excitement releases your energy. You trust it because you trust yourself. You give it meaning. You love it so you question yourself. You don't want your feelings running wild. You want to be sure your excitement supports your values. Most emotions have no consequence. They wait for your common sense to catch up so you can make a good decision. But how should you budget it? Where's the balance? You don't want to burn out and you don't want to die of boredom. You don't want to waste your time and you don't want to miss an opportunity. You want to be productive. You want to feel good. So keep questioning yourself, "Are you doing it right? What could make it better? Did you make any mistakes?" You have the ability to divide your consciousness while you do different things. Your thoughts question your experience. Your feelings question your will. Your soul questions Creation. They cover every thought you have. It's a lot to handle. You'd think you'd go crazy, and some people do.

It's not easy. Life's a challenge. That's why everyone has different talents. Some are good at analyzing things. Others can control their emotions. Some are close to God and others are born leaders. Talent is an asset. It supports you but it also directs you. It's your path of least resistance. You don't have to think about it. Like the carrot on a stick in front of the old mare's nose, you follow your nature. It could be financial success. It could be more time with your family. It's Love. Its negative expression is power. You think if you can control life you can control God. The confusion is thinking your power comes from superiority, me or you and not *us*. Consciousness is more than life. It answers to Eternity. It's easy for some and impossible for others. It's the opportunity in Creation. Eventually it makes sense and there's no penalty for getting it wrong. God's interested in your mistakes. It's the way God learns.

Real power is Love. When you look outside yourself for something better answered by your soul, all you can achieve is the illusion of success. What you identify with is never as important as your soul's experience. So it's what you tell yourself is important that matters. Like a child's drawing on the refrigerator door, Love makes everything beautiful. Fear's answer trusts what you control. It doesn't trust Love's generosity. It trusts ownership. Fear's uncertainty is answered by your self-respect. Your values support your self-respect. They're your hopes. Winning isn't getting more of what you already have. It's having what's important. The rules for getting it; that you have to decide.

You struggle with the possibilities. They're hard to control even with sensible values. Choices have costs. And there's a negative side if you get it wrong. No one wants rain at a picnic. Then how do you remove negative thoughts of failure and replace them with positive thoughts of success? You train yourself. You practice being positive. You tell yourself, "Yes, you can. You'll find a way. If it doesn't work, something better will happen." You release the negative thoughts of failure and define the situation in positive terms. You create positive habits that don't leave room for negative thoughts. And you keep doing it till it's second nature. You learn to trust yourself as a positive person. Self-respect does this for you. Love connects your self-respect to God's consciousness. Love connects everything.

"What's a good way to express your Love?" That's the question you ask every day. You want to be in harmony with Creation no matter how well you can carry a tune. If you don't have a beautiful voice, you can hum. You can whistle. You can stand in the back and mumble under your breath. You need that attitude. "There's always a way you *can* do it." Be confident in your ability to encourage your confidence. Trust Nature. No one wins every time. There are benefits to losing. You learn to improve yourself for the next opportunity. Life is competitive. That's the meaning of Nature. Confidence is a prize most people have to learn. Life's a maze and the only exit may be locked behind you, #debilitating disease. But you can still win. Maturity is your reward, a universal set of values you own. You have to experience life to see how things react, then you can adjust to it. Practice builds confidence and confidence frees you from old routines. It's simple as long as you refuse to fail.

SELF-RESPECT: THE SOLUTION TO UNSOLVABLE PROBLEMS

Confidence relies on having a positive opinion of yourself, win or lose. You can't beat yourself into submission and love yourself at the same time. There's no logic in it. You have to always love yourself. There's a difference between forcing yourself to do something and having a goal that inspires you to do it. You're not at war with yourself. You're a partner in your soul's ambition. Respect every part of yourself. Take responsibility but don't blame yourself. It's not a question of repaying a debt. There's nothing to even up. Life's an opportunity to improve your spiritual consciousness. That's all. You'd never make a bad decision if you knew the right answer. Your success depends on loving others, not the trendy perfections of the material world.

Others could suffer from your decisions. You can only hope for Peace in your sincerity. Forgive yourself and find remorse in your self-respect. It's the quiet way you love yourself. It's the conscious apology you make when you can't apologize in person. That's how you respect God. With a sincere heart you can trust the result even if you don't like it. Maybe you're in a war and your decision means civilians will suffer. Maybe you're an employer who has to fire a dependable employee because business is slow. Love is your guide. You would never do anything that would hurt someone if it could be avoided. Love carries the weight of hard choices. Make things right the best you can, then move on.

Your decisions are measured by your expectations. You don't need all the answers. Unexpected problems happen. Surprising opportunities appear. You project your vision and hope for the best. You question everything and try to improve it. Respect your decisions. Respecting yourself is the most important thing you can do. It's the most productive thing you can do. It's exciting to use your imagination and succeed. That's the point of creativity. When any human being creates a new design, *their* talent becomes part of *your* life. Their vision is an image of who you can be. They're saying, "I see this. Can you see it too?" You evolve by questioning everyone's vision. You don't need an artist's talent. You can contribute in your own way. Then you can show the world your perspective. It's the comfort in your self-respect despite life's tribulations.

You considered your options and made a decision. You know what you hope for, but it's easy to lose sight in the tug-of-war with your self-respect. Where does your self-respect meet with respect for others? These are the judgements you make every day. Life's struggle is finding that balance. You feed yourself and find a place to sleep. Then what? You wrestle with your conscience over what to do with yourself. When you succeed, you find satisfaction. When you give up, you have an open question. So keep questioning it. Keep questioning your feelings. What can you do that you like? You can do whatever you want as long as you're responsible to society. No matter how you picture your life, your self-respect will accommodate it. Every life has a formula for solving it. Your soul will tell you when you've succeeded.

Resources help, but most of life's problems are solved by ideas. There may be no easy way. The answer may require that you change the status quo. It's silly to curse your luck because you can't be a bird. You're not going to fly no matter how much you want to. But you can build an airplane. Nature's limits define you, but there's always a way even if you have to invent it. If you want to be a bird, that's not real. Being a pilot is real. You are who you are and you build your dream from there. You have God's help expanding your imagination into areas you never thought of. You may never reach your goal. That's not a problem. It's Nature. It's the will of Creation and you should accept it because there's always something better waiting for you.

You have to come to terms with Nature. It's not a problem unless you make it a problem. All answers share the consciousness of making the right connections. Life's a chasm between you and what you want. You need a way to get to the other side. It's as simple as a log bridge or as complex as convincing 100 million people to recycle their trash. If there's nothing in your environment that gives you what you want, then you have to find it somewhere else...or create it. Achievement is an attitude. It focuses on the creative power God gave you to change things. Respect that part of your nature. Love will always find a way.

Creativity is everybody's talent. It's your answer to every question, but it may be impractical. You have to consider reality. You have to keep at it till you have a working solution. It's not easy. Every answer is a link in the chain, but it's not one chain in a single line. It's a pile of chains, like a multi-dimensional spider's web. You can never be sure which thread will take you where you want to go. It's not meant to block you. It's meant to make you think. It's meant to make you use your creativity. It's designed to help you make choices that support your values. It tests your values under different

SELF-RESPECT: THE SOLUTION TO UNSOLVABLE PROBLEMS

conditions, because you learn something different from every experience. A solution needs attention or it can fail under the pressure of life's competition. That's why you have a gas gauge in your car. You don't want to run out of gas. Evolution travels a hundred directions before it moves forward an inch. Know what you want. See how close you can match it to reality. Question everything till all the parts fit. Then go forward and do it again.

You wouldn't cheat yourself and there's no reason to cheat anyone else. There's plenty for everyone. Desperation, the belief that it's okay to sacrifice your self-respect, means you give up. As a short term tactic it may fit your goal. Sometimes you have to stop and regroup. It doesn't mean you've lost as long as you respect yourself, keep your goal in mind, and keep your antennae tuned to new opportunities. Sometimes you have to work at a job you hate till you find one you like. You can excuse yourself and blame your circumstances, but you won't respect yourself till you make it right. Your soul only knows fairness on *its* terms. Fairness is the connection that makes you whole with Creation. That unity speaks to you when you pass a homeless person on the street or watch TV as some disaster destroys people's lives. You sympathize with them. You psychically want them to know that they're not alone. It happens every day. And it matters because you have to act on it.

Life's confusing for everyone. Through practice you learn to be a loving person. You know when things are wrong. You want to be a responsible person so you care about people. You hope every family teaches its children a productive way through life, to make a plan, and work at it. They don't teach that in school. School teaches the building blocks and natural order of things. It doesn't teach character. That you teach yourself. Character is how you balance your compromises with your values. It often gets delegated to religious training, but there are basic principles everyone can use without intruding on anyone. It's Love. It's personal responsibility. You must appreciate the freedom that comes from increasing your value, not the illusion of freedom that comes from doing nothing. With its eternal outlook your soul encourages you. It already has the answer. Its purpose is to help you reach your goal with your character intact. Thank God, your mistakes are forgiven.

No one has it all. There's always something missing. There's no benefit to having it all. In spirit you already have everything. There's always an aspect of life you're here to question. The life you choose is created from the values that attract you. Beauty is attractive. Safety is attractive. Control is attractive. Winning is attractive. The problem with riches is thinking that you're somehow deficient. Your car isn't cool enough or your hair could be straighter. Your style is old or life has no meaning if you can't eat at a trendy restaurant. Success tests your values. You have to be clear about your identity. There's the conundrum of who you'd like to be with; the attractive bimbo or the brilliant nerd. They may both be wonderful people; tolerant and supportive. It's how you value a person that defines your self-respect. Peace of mind is having what you tell yourself is important and knowing what you tell yourself is true.

So keep questioning yourself, "How will you pay your bills? Is your family okay? Are you in harmony with life? Are your aspirations valid?" You want to feel good about everything. You want to trust that you're using your opportunities. You want to believe that you respect your problems. That's all you can do. Life will show you if you're destined for greatness. Everyone doesn't win the gold medal. True greatness is your belief in yourself. It means you respect every thought that makes you who you are. Very little separates you from others. We all look the same. We all need Love. And everyone's doing their best to succeed.

Creativity means you can have anything you want. With money you can buy it. If you can create it another way you don't need the money. Falling in Love doesn't need money. Living in a vacation spot has all the advantages of a weekend holiday and you can have it every day. A cheap wine will get you just as drunk as fancy champagne. But social conflicts can't be solved if people don't respect each other. You have to nurture the balance of mutual respect. Where people have reasonable values you'll always find self-respect. To respect yourself without fighting for it is everyone's dream. When you have self-respect, problems solve themselves. Life naturally accommodates Love. Loving yourself is the easiest thing in the world because it's your decision. But life may not agree with you. It could demand more. Maturity doesn't need more. It respects the values that respect Love. That's why you keep asking yourself, "Did you do your best to be a loving person?"

Self-talk divides your consciousness. There's the everyday "You" that reacts to your feelings, and the spiritual "You" that requires that your values are

SELF-RESPECT: THE SOLUTION TO UNSOLVABLE PROBLEMS

supported by your actions. Love defines it all. Your job is to tie it together. Whatever you call it, there's a part of you aware of yourself and your ability to accept or reject your circumstances for whatever reason you want. As long as you know that, you can choose your priorities and change them as you like. That's your maturity. You always want the best value. Some people don't know any better. They're on automatic with the same values they've had for years. They cling to them because it's what they know. Right or wrong they're comfortable with them. They don't question it. It takes less work…and less confrontation with their feelings. To be your best takes courage. You can improve yourself if you make improving yourself a priority. Old habits retreat, but they always exist as a guide until you can find something better.

You have to want to be a better person. For all the disdain religions suffer, they're about how to be a better person. Religious attitudes grow with society because Love evolves. But how can Love's perfection be better? It looks for what it doesn't know. It wants to explain the eternal nature of the unknown. It's always whole but it's always changing. You change it. Religious ideas may be useful or just add to your confusion. It's a personal thing that depends on your perspective. There are many ways to do the same thing. Whatever happens, Love connects it. Everyone wants to feel good. Everyone questions how to do it. Religion helps. Philosophy helps. Education helps. Experience helps. Observation helps. Advice helps. Role models help. They're all perspectives from people who've been there. Then you have to decide what's important to you.

You talk to yourself. You listen to yourself. Then you make judgments. That's what it is to be a human being. You're always deciding what's best for you. You're always thinking (or really asking yourself) how to get what you want. It's your self-awareness, your self-respect. Like everyone, you have similar experiences and different experiences. Everything goes its own way so you need personal responsibility to make sure you get what you want. You're the one who'll change your life. What precedes every thought are the same questions, "Are you doing your best? Is it fair to everyone?" It would be simple if every question was the same but you're always in new situations with people you don't know. So what should you trust? Common sense is useful but emotion means you don't always use your common sense. So you keep asking, "How do I honor my self-respect when the results are so unpredictable?"

What often substitutes for self-respect is self-aggrandizement. It imagines its value more than what it really is. It's easily satisfied because the comparison comes from desire, not reality. It assesses responsibility where the only criterion is superiority. The same question you ask in traffic you ask in every relationship, "Who has the right of way?" You might applaud yourself for passing a slow driver or call yourself a "dumbass" when you miss your exit, but you're constantly making decisions on what you think you're responsible for. In this perpetual state of judgment you're also deciding what you think others are responsible for. Self-aggrandizement is a convenient opinion that always favors itself. It won't accept second best so it imagines a different reality. But it's a fearful thought. It feels good for the moment but it's confused. Don't count on other people accepting it. Life is more than wishful thinking. You have to perform. Better to depend on your self-respect. It trusts the truth and has your best interests at heart. It's fair and fairness has God's blessing.

What corrupts self-talk is thinking you're better than someone else and entitled to privileges they don't deserve. It fantasizes justifications for your superiority but in reality is a narcissistic illusion. Maybe you're more successful. Maybe you've been there longer. Maybe you're higher up the chain of command. It's the individuality of your consciousness thinking you deserve special treatment. Everyone has to compete. Everyone wants the best seat. That's the challenge of fairness. Are you willing to compromise your desire for the Love of humanity? A fair balance honors your self-respect because it trusts Creation's unity. Identifying with selfish fantasies creates conflicts because reasonable people believe they're important no matter where they stand in life's hierarchy. Whenever there's a threat to society, the rich and poor stand together. Division ends because everyone matters. Society matters. Civilization matters.

These are the values you weigh every day. Is a stranger's disdain a judgment on you as a person? Yes, it is. It's the battle for self-respect you fight for each day. It's how you measure your compromises. It's how you find peace with your neighbors. It's in the school yard and the courtroom. It's in insults and threats. It's judgmental. It challenges your common sense. It's someone else's

SELF-RESPECT: THE SOLUTION TO UNSOLVABLE PROBLEMS

idea of right and wrong...about you! It's a lack of confidence that believes your self-respect depends on someone else. Instead of trusting God, it descends into the raw competition of survival. If you believe that, then your self-talk depends on desperation. Is your situation hopeless or can you find another way. Protect your values. They're the essence of your self-respect. You'll need them if you want a good opinion of yourself. You spend a lot of time with your values. Don't waste it taking the easy way out.

The issue with avoiding a problem is your soul won't believe it. You can rationalize away your responsibilities but your soul knows the truth. You have to hide from the truth because your soul won't stop shouting it. It wants you to question your beliefs. It's how God gets your attention. God wants the truth so these are the questions God wants you to ask. God loves your thoughts, especially when you crave understanding. God knows the resentful thoughts you use to justify yourself. God knows your flawed solutions when you identify with a negative thought. God sees your self-pity when you believe the only one left to blame is God. When you tell yourself you're unworthy you ignore God's omnificence. God thinks you're the best, and there's nothing that can change that. You can question God's purpose but not its support. God loves you. It's the energy in everything. It's all the pieces and all they'll ever be. It's Peace. That's where you come from. That's where you make your contribution to Creation. God respects you so follow the leader and respect yourself.

You might have to realign your values. It takes time, maybe a lifetime, but what else have you got to do? Why do you think you're here, to have another slice of pizza? You talk to yourself to align your thoughts with your good intentions but it's your choice to involve God. God's Love energizes your thoughts. You have to trust it. You have to trust your faith will make it stronger. When does it start? It starts right away. How will you know it's happening? You'll feel good about yourself. When will it end? It never ends. You'll get lost at times because it's your right to make a bad decision, but it's also your right to make better decisions. Wherever you go, your faith will bring you back and God will be there waiting for you. When you think you have everything, God will drop a bomb in your lap just to see how you handle it. Life isn't all puppies and flowers. You'd lose interest in it if it was. Life is having victories as simple as choosing the right thing to say. It turns nervousness into tension, and tension builds strength. So be grateful for your challenges and enjoy God's support. It'll never let you down. Keep telling yourself that and a positive attitude will give you everything.

Imagining yourself in a conversation is a good way to focus your thinking. It helps you control your feelings because you won't be pressured by an unexpected question. You can comfortably imagine the possibilities. You can analyze your opinion under different conditions so you have an appropriate answer. Self-talk helps you decide what to say so you don't get lost in emotions. You want to say the right thing at the right time. You want to connect with the other person. You want to convince them that trusting you is a good decision. You want them to be comfortable with their decision. You could be asking to borrow their car or trying to think up an excuse for coming in late. It could take a week or just pop in your head. Then it becomes someone else's decision and all you can do is brace yourself for it. You hope for an agreement. Waiting for approval is one of the most stressful things there is. People may not agree, but they'll trust you when you prove you know what you're talking about.

Chapter 7
Confidence

Self-respect depends on your confidence. It's your belief that you'll be successful regardless of the obstacles. Your confidence knows life's unpredictable. It also knows you can master it. You don't always start at the beginning. You rely on your experience. You've learned things. You know how to win. You may fail but you always improve. You keep getting better. Then you can do things people who haven't made the effort can't do. Look at all those stunt riders on TV. They stand on the saddle, hang from the horse's neck, and ride two horses at a time. They do incredible things. They may have started years ago. They may have a natural affinity for animals. Whatever talent they have, they still practice till they can do it every time without falling. And they fell plenty of times. Confidence takes experience. That's why old people don't worry. They know things will work out one way or the other. Even the old concert master still practices. The saying stands, "Practice makes perfect."

Some things you can't do. Life has its limits. You may be smart enough but not have the training. You don't want your doctor to fix your car. You may be in good shape but not have the size. Maybe you're too big to be a jockey. You can do anything as long as you respect your limits. If you want to compete you have to work at it because there are people just like you who want the same thing. You do your best. You keep improving. Maybe you're in the media but there's too much competition where you are. So you move where there's less competition till you're good enough to win in a bigger market. You groom yourself for success. Your skills increase and your confidence grows. Confidence doesn't guarantee you success. It prepares you for it.

A talent is God's gift but a skill you have to learn. It can be anything. It can be plumbing or practicing the law. You learn by experience and you learn by studying; a condensed kind of experience. You can create a skill no one else has, like a unique bowling stance or a mental trick for remembering people's names. Skill and experience are the same. You teach yourself or you learn it from others. There's the story of Harpo Marx, the silent Marx brother, who excelled at playing the harp. He was self-taught. Eventually he hired a concert harpist to tutor him so he could be a better player. In a short time Harpo realized he knew more than the expert and let him go. The expert was more intrigued learning what Harpo found on his own than by what he could teach him. Your skills have no bounds. You're only limited by the questions you ask, "Will it work? Can you do it?" And the answer is always, "Try."

You're naturally wary. Your survival instinct kicks in like a startled dog. You ask yourself, "Is something wrong? Am I safe?" It's easy when you know what you're doing, but you don't always know what you're doing. You're always finding yourself in new situations. You want reliable answers and you want them now. You want to trust yourself. Everyone's not designed to challenge a mystery. It takes work. The more you work at it, the better you get. Your confidence grows. If you're not born with confidence, you can learn it. Confidence is a skill too. It's frustrating looking at your engine wondering why your car doesn't work. Most people have no idea how to fix a car. Is it a loose wire or a worn part? And what's that noise? Worse than searching for an answer, you don't even know what you're looking at. You don't know if that part will break if you turn it too far. A rusty bolt will break for a skilled mechanic too. When you trust your skills, you're confident not perfect. Confidence accepts Nature's ups and downs. Nature goes its way and you go yours. Your task is to bring them together. And it often depends on how you feel at the moment.

A skill has two parts. The first is identifying the problem. The second is knowing how to fix it. The first part is diagnosis. You want to understand the problem so you can trace it back to the cause. Then you can eliminate the cause and repair the problem. Why doesn't the light work? Why did your customer grimace at that point in your presentation? Why are you sick? Something changed. Something was working and then it stopped working. How can you get it to work again? What adjustment can you make? Will you need help? All skills start with evaluation. What's wrong? Can it be fixed? Is it redeemable or do you need a new one? You may understand it completely

SELF-RESPECT: THE SOLUTION TO UNSOLVABLE PROBLEMS

until you come across something you've never seen before. Then your skills become experience. It's the old joke, "That person forgot more than you'll ever know." The funny thing is a lot of that is true.

Experience grows over time. Why does the roof leak? What do you know about fixing roofs? How many roofs have you fixed? Two or two hundred? How many variations of the problem have you seen? Experience is more than learning from books or interning with a master. Experience comes from practice. Experience is self-taught. It respects everything you know and accepts there's always room to know more. The same issue comes up in different ways so you know how to handle it. Sometimes it's confusing. It's not that you don't have the skill. It's that you haven't seen the problem enough to know how it might react...and so how to fix it. Through experience you've probably considered the problem before. That's why doctors have specialties. They don't diminish the advantage of having more experience in one area. Their job is too important for them not to know *everything*. So you have cardiologists and psychiatrists. It's good for them because they can focus on the intricacies of what interests them. Do you want someone working on your car who fixes ten cars a day or one that fixes one car a month?

Your first responsibility is to yourself. Whatever you do, you want to do it well. You don't have to know everything. You have to know what's important. So you ask questions. You get advice. You compare the costs and benefits. "What would work best?" You're always asking that question. You still need confidence even if it means following advice from someone you don't know, like a new dentist. Your confidence in yourself extends to your confidence in others. You're always the judge. Whose advice should you trust? It's never a substitute for your trust in yourself. It's still your responsibility. You may be confused. You may be afraid. Respect your good intentions. Respect your good nature. Confidence aligns with your self-respect. You'll get it right most of the time, at least from your point of view. And forgive your mistakes. Sincerity is all you need to justify yourself.

Confidence doesn't equal self-respect. It's an extension of it. Self-respect guides it. It includes every experience you've ever had. When you add spiritual consciousness, you create your self-respect. Your free will defines it so be proud of yourself. Self-respect is an achievement. It's your support for yourself. You control everything when you respect yourself. You want to win when you're supposed to win and you want to win when it's unlikely you'll win. The result often depends on things you can't control (like competition) even when you do your best. God has a plan. Some days it's your turn to win and some days it's the other person's turn. Confidence depends on faith. Faith is a skill too. You have to practice it. You have to risk your beliefs. Religious rules don't matter unless you want them to. Your trust in God matters. It takes confidence in God before you can be confident in yourself. There's too much resistance in life. You need help. You don't turn God on and off with a switch. You build the bond through your sincerity. God replies with its reliability. The good news is it gets easier as you go.

You can do anything. You'll get most things right and what you don't you'll fiddle with till you do. You know when you're successful. You like how it feels and you applaud yourself for your accomplishment. Confidence and self-respect support each other. The more confident you are, the more you respect yourself. The more you respect yourself, the more confident you are. They grow together. Practice and you'll own them. Confidence can be your reality. Life is confusing but your confidence doesn't care. It takes on all comers. It takes on every situation. Your confidence wants what's best for you and believes you can have it. You know what winning means. Trust yourself that you can put the pieces together. Your confidence knows when it's aligned with your self-respect because you find your Peace there.

Faith is hard to accept. You've had so many disappointments. You still have to decide what faith means to you. You can ignore it but why turn away help? But you want proof. For someone at the end of their rope, a belief is something to trust when there's nothing left. If you're doing well, there's no need for anything else. Most people believe things get better when they work at it. From a religious standpoint, God's kindness may be something you think you can trade for if you pray enough. You can't avoid a problem. They'll find you wherever you are. Some days you wake up with a cold. Life's maintenance never ends. It's hard. It's your responsibility and you want to do well. Faith tests you when life is the hardest because it wants you to trust it. Love's protection is always with you. God commands your attention through your problems, but what good is faith if you can't control it? You control faith through your trust in God's purpose. You never control the outcome.

SELF-RESPECT: THE SOLUTION TO UNSOLVABLE PROBLEMS

It's your job to explore the outcome. You can only hope something good comes from it.

Faith feels good. It's a comfort. It's dependable. You know you're not alone. When you think you're exhausted, faith stands up to support you. It's your trust in Love...and Love always wins. God wants to be your partner. Faith seals the deal. You can smile at the worst circumstances because there's nothing life can take from you. In passing, you release all attachments. Then you can honor the Peace in your soul. Faith doesn't judge you. It accepts you and lovingly responds. Then the confidence you practiced in life, you won't need anymore. You'll be free in Creation. You'll venture out as the true soul you are. And you'll know it. So forgive your regrets and trust that you did your best. Faith loves you even when you question it.

Until then, you'll depend on your self-respect. It trusts that you care about yourself. Confidence is your plan for winning. It supports you when you try something new. It's your belief that you'll succeed. It's not an act though sometimes while you're learning you have to play the part. The danger is the convenience in a false impression instead of doing the work. You don't want to rely on an act no matter how convincing it is. Eventually it'll show its weakness. Real confidence doesn't depend on success. It trusts your self-respect is enough. Confidence is a positive attitude. You may have goals but God chooses your challenges. Confidence trusts the wisdom in God's plan. There are times you'll get knocked on your butt. Confidence means a failure won't change your good opinion of yourself. Your self-respect will simply tell you to find another way.

Confidence sends you in the right direction. It's more than an attitude. It's your spiritual nature. You can train yourself to be confident. It's not a secret. You encourage the bond between you and God. You trust together you can handle anything. You're right to be concerned but don't worry. When you're confident, there's nothing to worry about. You learn to trust success however it comes. Confidence respects the opportunities in life's challenges. You won't always win no matter how confident you are. But you can always respect yourself for your desire to win. Confidence is emotional. It's your free will wanting to win. You can want something so much that you push yourself past your limits. When you do more than common sense says you can, you express confidence.

Controlling your emotions is the key, so be careful how you trust your feelings. Elation and despondency both ignore common sense. The contest is never over. That's Eternity's message. How many sporting events have you seen won by a single point when the team was down miserably at the half? What seemed like a rout turns 180 degrees. It affects both teams; those who thought they had the game in their pocket and those who thought the game was hopelessly lost. Your free will is a positive force in Creation. Every breath affirms Love's purpose. Life can be miserable for a long time. How you use that time is the way you build your confidence. If you can shake the misery for a moment then you win that moment. You're not doomed to misery. You're guaranteed Love. How you adapt your feelings is the job. You succeed in your hopes so don't beat yourself up over problems. Respect your confidence knowing, with God, your victory is certain.

How do you feel confident? What does confidence feel like? You know you don't want to be afraid. Fear helps you recognize a danger, but you wouldn't want to avoid your responsibility because you were afraid. You want to accept the facts and win despite your fear. Confidence focuses your attention. It's your belief that you can understand any problem and solve it. Your confidence believes you're a sensible person. You may or may not be. Being honest is the first step to trusting yourself. You have to trust your nature. You have your own way of doing things. Confidence has a different persona for each of us. The common thread is it sees you succeeding before you even start.

You trust your senses to recognize things. You trust your body because it's your ability to do things. You trust your thinking because it helps you understand things. You trust your feelings because they tell you if those things are good for you. You trust your soul because it connects you to Love and Love connects everything. And you trust your creativity because you're an expert at imagining things. It's all there. When you do the same thing over and over you gain confidence. You know how to do it. You trust you can do it. You can hammer a nail or paint your nails. You know what should happen because you've done it before. It's second nature. But that's not confidence. That's experience. Confidence is meeting the unknown. Can you convince someone to buy what you're selling? Who knows? You have to try if you want

SELF-RESPECT: THE SOLUTION TO UNSOLVABLE PROBLEMS

an answer. You have to believe you can. You have to respect your ability. You have to believe whatever happens you'll keep trying.

Confidence includes your beliefs. It's how you negotiate life. It's not whether or not the water comes on when you turn the faucet. It's your commitment that one way or another you're going to wash your hands. It respects your purpose. It knows your priorities. It's the subconscious sense that you prepared the best you can and you'll do what it takes to succeed. There are too many variables to guarantee success every time. Confidence believes your intention will succeed no matter what happens. It trusts you'll work out the details. It trusts Nature. It trusts God. It trusts your soul's purpose. It doesn't eliminate your doubts. It builds on your beliefs.

You can change your beliefs whenever you want. Confidence is a belief. It's an insight into how you value yourself. It helps you imagine life's uncertainties. It helps you analyze your priorities. Confidence doesn't just happen. You have to test it and see how it does. You want to trust yourself. Confidence grows with your successes, even as small as changing a light bulb. The light goes on and the lamp doesn't explode. It proves you can do anything because you trust yourself. Confidence can't be rationalized. You have to feel it. It's a belief not an understanding. You can practice it though until you believe it. You can learn to trust yourself. It makes sense but it's more than logic. Maybe it's calculable in some universal algorithm but you don't need God's wisdom to be confident. You already have the tools. It's the belief in your soul that you were born to win.

Feelings are your subconscious guide. They're your support. "Do this. It's good for you." What's "good" changes with how you perceive your needs. Your confidence wants your attention. It relies on facts, not wishful thinking. It focuses on what's important now and how it could affect you in the future. Understanding the problem is the key to solving it. That's why you're good at asking questions. You want to know what the problem is asking for. It doesn't mean you have a perfect plan for every possibility. It means you respect your common sense. It means you trust your purpose. That's why you prepare for situations that probably will never happen; like a flood or someone sticking a microphone in your face and asking you a personal question. That's the benefit of preparation; knowing what you're going to do *before* it's time to do it. Training supports your confidence. It's the skill to avoid panic and let your confidence take charge.

Success often depends on your confidence. Confidence comes from believing in yourself. In life you expect anything can happen so you prepare for it. You keep a flashlight close by in case the lights go out. Confidence is more. It's emotional preparation. It's the comfort in knowing you have a working flashlight. It's an instinct you develop. It makes sense. You answer to yourself. You want to trust you can solve a problem or call someone who can. You don't know everything. There's always the unpredictable. If you're a plumber, you may understand the principles of plumbing but you don't know if that old pipe will break if you turn it too far. Confidence is a starting point. Even an experienced plumber may have to go to the store several times before they have all the parts they need. It's normal. Confidence expects questions. Confidence doesn't mean starting perfectly. It means ending successfully.

Confidence goes hand-in-hand with self-respect. It has to support your values. You're alone no matter how much help you get. So you have to be confident for reasons that make sense to YOU. Advice is a gift as long as it respects what *you* want. Confidence frames your self-respect. It supports your importance. It cares about you. You have to trust your sincerity that you're making the right choice for the right reason. You want to feel good about yourself even when you're disappointed. Your confidence may not change anything. For whatever reason, you just can't do it. Then your self-respect takes over. Self-respect believes in your perfection as God's creation. Free will means you decide the rules. The only rule you can never change is you must respect Love.

Self-respect doesn't depend on confidence. Confidence is your trust in self-respect. It doesn't depend on what you want. It depends on getting started. You have to believe you can do something even if it turns out you can't. Life has too many obstacles. Everyone has a bad day or their skills aren't up to the task. Your confidence accepts this. Its question is, "Are you ready to begin?" Confidence is your emotional interpretation of your chance for success. The details don't matter. Your objective is to succeed whatever you do. It's the certainty in your belief regardless of the issues. Don't just respect who you are. Trust who you are. Don't rely on over-the-top enthusiasm or clever remarks. Confidence is your ability to succeed with what you have.

SELF-RESPECT: THE SOLUTION TO UNSOLVABLE PROBLEMS

You get to the point where success is the only thing you'll accept. Every contest is a series of plays and you don't have to win them all to win the game. Maybe you don't feel confident. Maybe you're afraid you'll make a mistake. How can you be confident if you're confused? Knowing what you're doing helps. Knowing why you're doing it helps. Having the right tool helps. Training helps. Experience helps. Having a clear goal helps. Having a sensible plan helps. Resources help. That's all logical but where's your confidence? It comes when you trust your fate. It's not bravado. It's faith. When you want something, maybe you can reach it or maybe you first have to move closer. How many times have you been driving and dropped something on the floor of the passenger's seat. You can stretch to get it, but it's really too far and too dangerous to try while you're driving. So you pull over and if you still can't reach it, you get out and go through the passenger's door. Sometimes the issue is distance and sometimes the issue is time. You always knew you'd get it but you had to be patient. Everything works that way. You want something but you don't want to overstretch and hurt yourself when all you have to do is wait for a better time.

How do you trust a belief? First, don't assume you're right. Your self-respect depends on it so being confident matters. Your welfare depends on it. The alternative is doubt and you don't want to constantly battle your anxiety. You want to enjoy life's mystery. Your creativity helps you organize the unknown; whether it's backtracking to find your cellphone or figuring a good place to meet a mate. The unknown is an exotic game. Sometimes you play with strangers and sometimes you play with God. In a way, you make the rules so it's a little different for each of us. Fairness is the challenge of civilization. Your confidence grows with the rules you trust. But, there's no guarantee. You can keep your car in perfect condition but there's no accounting for that unseen nail that gives you a flat tire. That's life. You can just as easily run into an old friend you haven't seen in twenty years. Some days are sunny and some days it rains. Like it or not, your soul needs both to keep itself balanced. You do what you can to improve your chances, but your confidence doesn't rely on results alone. It trusts Love will solve the problem.

Things can change unexpectedly so learn to rely on your confidence. It's your belief in your ability regardless of the situation. It's your belief that you'll always do well and land on your feet. Your confidence loves you. Like the children's game "Chutes and Ladders," a roll of the dice sends you in a new direction. For a confident person it's a new starting point. You haven't lost anything. The play simply shifted and changed your point of view. That's all. Sometimes it's worse, sometimes it's better, but that's the game. The question is, "How can you win from where you are now?" Your goal is the same so you make a new plan. You may think your original plan was perfect, but life has as many opportunities in the unexpected as it has for problems. So don't worry. Your confidence only cares for what helps you.

Being sure is the first step. Right or wrong, you know where you are. You can always change your mind. It's important to grow with it. Life's confusing for everyone. Confusion can go back to your childhood when a lack of confidence was instilled in you by people who didn't have much themselves. This is the work of confidence. It helps you mature. It believes you can do whatever you want when you're honest with yourself. Self-respect wants you to win. You may not win every time but you must always win when your character's at stake. Experience is what you wanted in the first place. Your soul wants you to be a better person. But life can make you feel like a victim. The #1 confusion is to believe you should suffer. That's negative thinking. You're prepared to fail before you even have a problem. Then you create justifications to diminish your hopelessness and you wind up chasing your tail. Don't judge yourself harshly. The door to Peace may be small, but it's always open. You may have to accept your confusion until you can trust your judgment. Till then, pay attention.

Where does a lack of confidence come from? Your limited experience trained you to believe it. It's become so ingrained you barely know you have a choice. You do have a choice and it only takes a minute to change it. It's an attitude and you can have a different attitude. Any idea attached to your thoughts takes work to change. Your job is to do the work. It's a thought and you can change your thought. You can change your mind. Seeing its value is the essence of self-respect. You can have years of bad habits but the process to fix it is simple. You change your focus from the problem to your reaction. Then you focus on a positive result. What are you thinking? If you only come up with negative thoughts then you're doing well. You've identified the problem. Now you can begin your transformation. You're not judging yourself. Negative beliefs are a normal condition, like having a rash. There's

SELF-RESPECT: THE SOLUTION TO UNSOLVABLE PROBLEMS

nothing wrong with you as a human being. When you appreciate the process, you'll see how right you are and the rash will go away.

Routines let your mind run free. The problem is negative thoughts can become false beliefs. You come to believe every outcome will fail. The solution is to believe you'll succeed. You have to retrain your mind and change your beliefs. Dismiss failure and expect success. It takes practice. It takes acceptance to keep trying after you've failed. First you have to see a thought is negative and then stop thinking it. You have to find a positive way to express the same idea. It takes patience. It can take years, but it's like a snowball rolling downhill. It gains momentum with every positive thought. Your choice is simple. Be hopeful or be miserable. Which do you think feels better? Some negative thoughts underlie all your thinking. They're important but they're easier to change. Removing one negative attitude can release huge amounts of positive energy, like admitting to a fear of failure that makes you hesitant to try new things. Other negative thoughts are specific to a relationship and need fearless honesty to dig out the truth. Positive thinking highlights your self-respect. It says that you're willing to trust Creation.

You have to train yourself. It can take years but the benefits are immediate. You feel good about yourself. You have more control. Your confidence grows and you trust yourself. Negative thoughts become bumps in the road. They block you but there's no real problem. Like a pothole, you just walk around it. It's only a thought. It's not real. As you mature, you evaluate which thoughts are worthwhile and which ones aren't. You learn to accept the pain in facing an unpleasant truth. Life can be hard for the positive thinker too. But even that recedes when you trust yourself. Whatever happens, accept the benefit and move on. You can't move past a problem till you accept it. Admitting the small pains encourages you to uncover the pains that have you stuck. Then you mature and work past them all till the pain is gone completely. You have to be willing and you have to be brave. You have to be confident you can do it...because you can.

The challenge is how to control your feelings. It's a skill you have to learn. Your emotions decide your compromises. Disappointments can be traumatizing. Escape may be impossible. Your soul urges you on but self-preservation tells you to "avoid the risk." You have to get by so you form emotional callouses to deaden the pain. In the same way a callous protects a farmer's hands from the pain of hard work you form emotional callouses to protect your feelings in relationships you can't leave, like being a parent or a spouse. It's easy to get stuck. You feel like a prisoner, frustrated and hopeless. It's a common challenge and you have to find your way through it. That's life. You're always looking for peace and harmony. You're always looking for Love. I'm sorry it's not easier but it's worth it.

You can't avoid life's ups and downs. Success is about being happy with yourself. That's what you need wherever you are. After the battles you still have to find peace with yourself. Relationships are opportunities. No matter how rough it gets, at least you have the opportunity to be a parent, a spouse, spend time by yourself, work on a team, work your butt off and win, work your butt off and lose, enjoy your culture, express your sexuality, and question your soul every step of the way. It's everything you could ask for. Every time you deal with something, you can win. A positive answer doesn't come from a negative attitude. It comes from a confident attitude.

Chapter 8
There's nothing wrong with you.

You want to do the right thing, but you don't always know the right thing to do. Maybe the right thing is taking a risk. It may not be a real risk but you think it is and it's what you think that matters. What you believe is your reality. So it's important to know what you can do in the environment you find yourself. You have to be honest with yourself. If you have a question, it's important to verify the details so you're confident with the answer. You rely on facts. The truth is in how you weigh the facts. You have to judge how the facts fit and identify the values they create. Then you can arrange the pieces to favor what you want. Wherever you are, you want to win. You may make a bad choice but you should never be surprised by something you should know. Regardless of what the world tells you, you're responsible for your choices. Wishful thinking isn't facts. You have to deal with what's real. You may be closer to winning than you think.

Your self-respect defines your beliefs. You have an image of success then you arrange your life to match it. So you wear a certain style to present yourself in a certain way. Your self-respect accepts you for who you are and supports who you want to be. Your self-respect includes your values. It helps form your opinion of right and wrong. Some values you expect everyone to accept. The Golden Rule and Ten Commandments are good examples of respectable social standards. Then there are the cultural rules that respect the differences in societies, like its religious holidays. Everyone shares the same desire for a society they can depend on. You know when to cheer and when to cry because you accept that you're part of it...and it's part of you.

Once you meet your responsibilities you can do whatever you like. You can live the solitary life of a scholar or join an expedition and scour the desert for treasure. The desire to live a full life is the same for everyone, but we all go about it in different ways. Both seek knowledge; one by reinterpreting existing knowledge in the safe environment of a secure room while the other faces the unpredictable challenges in the field but also enjoys the opportunity to be the first to see a new discovery. While in the same race, they go about it differently. One's not better than the other and both wind up in the same place. The difference is in how it appeals to their nature. Some like the activity; hiking through the sand looking for a lost civilization, while the others find peace in the mental exercise spending long nights struggling to read some forgotten language. Regardless of their styles, they both want the answer.

Life must respect you or you'll think it's unfair. You accept it because you like most things about it. With so many opinions you want a safe place in the chaos. You engage life every day as it starts and stops, whirls and twirls, till everything's a blur. Hopefully, it stops long enough for you to see it clearly and make a plan. Awareness begins your self-control. You can't stop the chaos so you have to live with it without hating it. People have different attitudes. Some follow rigid disciplines and others have no idea what's going on and walk into walls every day. Your question should always be, "Did you do the right thing?" then "What can you do better?" It focuses on what you want and where you set your limits. Then how are you supposed to find the right answer? It happens over time. You take a step back and see how you feel. Are your feelings appropriate? They can have a life of their own unrelated to what's going on. Self-awareness is half the battle. Controlling your feelings is the other half.

Your emotions guide your thoughts. They express your values. Values are the relative importance you give anything in a specific situation. You're a human being in a relationship with God. You can deny it but you can't avoid it. Every part of you includes God's energy. It's always changing so you're always adapting. But there's one thing that never changes. It's the enduring connection of Love. You love everything and everything loves you. It's the unified consciousness of God beyond your personality. It's the balance of Creation epitomized by you. Your spiritual connection includes your unending questions, "What should you do? What do you owe? Will others agree?" You climb that mountain every day. Sometimes you succeed. Sometimes you fail. But you're always learning. You're always questioning.

SELF-RESPECT: THE SOLUTION TO UNSOLVABLE PROBLEMS

You may not be interested in how things work. You may just want more stuff. But winning isn't just having more. It's knowing more. Everyone wants to move forward so you have to keep asking yourself, "Which way is "forward?" Life doesn't move in a straight line. It's just easier to see it that way; first, second, third. It's simple and direct. Life is more like intersecting spheres working as intricate gears in a complex machine, but instead of gears your thoughts and feelings revolve in every direction at once; sometimes by choice, sometimes by accident, but always with God's direction. Your Peace is in how you adapt to the motions. A balanced life is an acceptable average of good and bad experiences. It's what you like because you designed it. There's the proverbial story about the hard-working business person who never sees their kid in the school play. They're always working because there are bills to pay. Finding the balance between the practical side of paying the bills and the emotional side of supporting a loved one is an important challenge. You meet it by being creative and accepting responsibility. Work is work but life is more work.

Embrace your creativity. It's a better investment than hard work alone. It won't risk your future if you take time to share an ice cream with your kid. It'll find time for everything without being a burden. Your priorities change every minute. If you have time to sit in traffic then you have time to do something you like. Many of your values come from someone trying to sell you something. That's okay. It's business. Everyone has bills. But your decisions, even with your compromises, must support YOU. Any offer must prove itself on *your* terms. Accept reasonable guidance but be wary of being manipulated...even by your own illusions. Making good decisions is your life's work. It takes time and attention. It takes self-control. Having a car you can't afford lacks the self-respect in being able to pay for it. Self-respect knows its limits. You can't ignore a personal responsibility just because it's easier. You're the one who pays for everything, so be fair to yourself. If it's your responsibility you're going to pay for it one way or the other.

Fulfillment means finding your personal balance. It's the happy life you juggle every day. You can live in a mansion, but then you have to accept living with the maintenance people who take care of your mansion. Or you could have a long commute to a job that pays you well. There's always a trade-off. Self-respect comes from your willingness to evaluate your situation and find ways to improve it. You can take classes for a new career or for the joy of learning. You can wake up early to exercise so you don't take time from your day. You value your time then distribute it to meet your goals. You respect yourself knowing your sacrifices are the way you pay for your happiness. Mass consciousness has the usual prizes. You have to decide if they're what *you* want. Are they worth the effort? Is life more than pizza and shiny things? You're not a kid anymore. You know enough to make mature decisions. You don't have to be a star in the movies. You can be a star in the Universe.

You can ignore society. You can challenge its traditions. Traditions represent a society's values. They remember what people admire most about themselves. At best, traditions share a positive opinion. It's a family wedding, a college reunion, or wearing the team colors on game day. It's a unifying parade. Traditions inspire you to do your best because you represent your community. They must be flexible enough to welcome a new idea and firm enough to withstand misguided adventures. They support Love. Life is Love's growth. It's growth for you and growth for your community. It shouldn't be a change for change's sake. It should be an improvement. Traditions are a community's sense of its enduring value. It's not about individual personalities. It's how each personality is respected as part of the group.

A tradition shares the Love embraced in that tradition. You can be as hip as you like and still enjoy a corny tradition, like the hardened marine who dresses up like Santa Claus for the kids' toy drive. But what happens when you're uncomfortable with a tradition? What if you realize it's disrespectful? People don't always know what's disrespectful in society. They know what they're taught and they know Love. But you can't fool your soul. The agreements that created the social balance may not be valid anymore. All people know is what their self-respect tells them. Common sense should decide the compromise. There must be give and take on all sides to make it socially acceptable. All opinions must be considered to establish an equitable decision. That's what civilization is for, deciding what's fair. You're a human being so you're a social being. Cultures create opportunities for everyone. Each generation has to decide what's fair on its own terms. Cultures are alive. They're growing. The thing with a tradition is you have to accept you're part of it. It has to live up to your values to make it worthy of your self- respect.

SELF-RESPECT: THE SOLUTION TO UNSOLVABLE PROBLEMS

There are many traditions: national traditions, cultural traditions, and religious traditions. It's different people sharing one identity. The lesson is you're not alone. Your experiences tie us together. You know what to expect so you trust it. It's Nature's way of expressing God's support. You compromise some of your free will and it supports you as long as you participate. It's the old neighborhood. Whether it's a good memory or not you never get it out of your system. You may have long-established traditions but you'll join the next generation in interpreting them. Things change so it's important to have reliable values. There are the high ideals that attract you to a tradition and you must accommodate the human shortcomings in a group. The redeeming quality of a tradition is you respect yourself when you share it.

You're accepted by the group and expected to support it. You do what you can. You make phone calls or put away chairs. You help raise money or wear a button that represents a positive image to the community. You promote the group. You make yourself valuable. What do you get for your trouble? You get the group's support. You're gifted with its traditions whether you're a sports fan cheering on the team or celebrating a work anniversary with your co-workers. A tradition doesn't need a hundred years of history. It's in the routines that mark life's everyday events. "Didn't we do that last year? That was great. Let's do it again." You have the annual holiday party or the family gets together for a wedding. They're unifying experiences. They may seem trivial but they're important because they communicate a common ideal. The challenge is, "How do you maintain your personal values within a tradition?" Those family battles over old slights show how hard it can be.

You respect yourself through your values. You respect yourself when you're sure you're doing the right thing. It gives you the right to wonder why things are the way they are and how they could be better. Everything doesn't have to be a battle. You want peace when you compromise yourself in a marriage or a job. You want to be confident your compromise is worth the agreement. You share most of the same values with everyone. It's common sense. But you have your priorities. Are you playing golf this weekend or helping out at church? You want to feel good whatever it is. Even if you like fishing, you wouldn't want to do it in the rain.

You do what you like. Sharing what you do is the way you survive. You want to love your life. A bad marriage or bad job can taint everything you do. You want the peace to explore yourself. You want to trust yourself. But what if you can't? Can you still respect yourself? Some things you're not designed to do. You may be too small to be a football player or too nervous to be a performer. But there are many things you do well. You could be a hard worker or a dedicated friend. Society prizes money and sex. It's a compulsion. It's the essence of survival. There's always room for a bargain where money and sex are at stake. That's the business of life. It's not always a Love for humanity that brings us together. People take care of themselves first. The good thing about Love is there's plenty for everyone. It's the essence of your being but you can't force it. You have to go meet it. You have to choose it.

You know Love. It's how you measure your relationships. The question is, "What's the best way to express Love?" How do others express their Love? How do you express Love in a conflict? These are the questions for a civilized consciousness. Whatever you decide, there's nothing wrong with you. You're entitled to your values. To have self-respect that supports your values. If you don't, you can get lost in a fog of regrets. Love fits you perfectly. People may tell you there's something wrong with you or imply it in the way they treat you. Fortunately, it has no effect unless you let it. 99% of life can be tolerated...or should be. It's rare that you have to call in an air strike to justify your opinion. If you do, then you have to deal with the responsibility that comes with increasing the tension. You may have to. You want fairness and sometimes you must demand it. Life's a balance of energy. If you want more, then give more. Create an imbalance in the Universe that must find a way to give that energy back to you. Like everyone else, you have a right to it.

Injustice is real. You often have to walk the line between self-respect and what you're willing to compromise to survive. Every situation must be measured on its merits. What's important is how you feel about yourself. You're the one with the answer. Are you living up to your values? Are you living up to your responsibilities? Consider everything. Are you being fair? The answers define you. Are you doing enough? Are you supporting yourself? Are you supporting the community? Are they supporting you? You ask the same questions with every thought you have. That's what you're supposed to do; question the choices that support your values. The tricky part is how to set priorities when everything keeps changing. You need a core value to simplify things. That's why Love matters. Everything boils down to how you care

SELF-RESPECT: THE SOLUTION TO UNSOLVABLE PROBLEMS

about yourself and how you care about others...Love. It's the measure of your thinking, so it's the measure of your life.

That's your challenge; to respect what you know. First you need to know what you want. You have to contend with everyone's values plus the cultural differences that define your priorities. It takes maturity. But what if you're not mature? Then rely on the Golden Rule. The Golden Rule is common sense. *Do unto others as you would have them do unto you.* It's simple. It relies on deciding right or wrong in light of what you know. It underscores all your relationships. It implies that you know the right thing to do because you know what's important to you. The hard part is making compromises with your priorities. How can you satisfy everyone all the time? Add a fear of failure and it's nearly impossible. That's why life's a burden. It's confusing. There's more than one right path. That's why growing up is so hard. Everyone's trying to define themselves in an environment designed to test them. Think of a time when you had to wait in line for tickets to a movie and you finally got to the box office and all the seats were taken. Life's the grown up version of musical chairs. No matter who you are, sometimes you're out.

You want to look good. You want to enjoy the kindness of friends. It might mean playing in the boss's foursome or having lunch with the head of the Human Resources department. You want to be popular with people who can help you. Wherever you are, from the school yard to the board room, you want to be liked. You want to be the person others want to know. You want to be included. You want your interests considered. The message of not being included is there's something wrong with you. You know your shortcomings or at least you know the shortcomings society avoids. Everyone follows the trend. It's the leading edge of the social adventure. It's where the winners are. It's often blind luck how well you match a social ideal. Sometimes it's beauty. Sometimes it's knowledge. Being a good worker isn't enough. Success is equally measured by the strength of your social skills. You want people to like you. People who like you trust you. When people trust you, they'll help you.

You must be positive because you have to adapt. You have to know your choices. You have to be realistic. Life's not all sunny days. There are times you have to make decisions you don't like. There are times the storms of human nature will confront you. It could be a community crisis or someone you Love who's struggling. Usually it's just another drudgery like the inexperienced salesperson you're asking for help. Most people are reasonable. They want to help. They're like you. They have people they love. They have a spiritual sense of themselves. They want to do the right thing then go on with their lives. Most people are fair but not everyone. Some are weak and make up for their weakness abusing others. They deny Love and the courtesy that makes us whole. They'll tell you something's wrong with you and you won't get what you want unless you do what they say. It's the unpleasant environment of unfairness and you have to deal with it the best you can. Avoid it if possible. You don't want to spend more time then you have to with that kind of person.

Everything you do includes your self-respect. Then along comes someone who tells you there's something wrong with you. There's no Love in ignorance. It's selfish. Guilt is a selfish attitude confronted by the truth. At its worst it becomes jealousy. You become a convenient target for someone's self-serving thinking. It can cause problems. People gossip and they might gossip about you. Gossip isn't the truth. It's a creative interpretation of someone's opinion of what could be an interesting truth. It's 80% socializing and 20% fact. But it might cost you that promotion you're working on. Backstabbing is a common problem and you'll be the last to know. A backstabber won't confront you. They'll confront others about you. There's not much you can do about a competitive person who doesn't like you. You're probably doing your best right now. So you have to speak up. You have to be your own cheerleader. Most people focus on the last thing they've heard. You want it to be the truth. You have to challenge every lie or risk it becoming something worse.

There's nothing wrong with you. Appreciate yourself as a human being. Everyone has foibles and there are plenty to go around. Character faults are part of life. They color your challenges. They personalize your life. You have to find a way to accommodate them to be a better person. They bring out your creative nature in the way you adapt. The game is to improve yourself despite your faults. It's not hating yourself because you're not "perfect." It's rising above your faults. There's nothing wrong with being human. It has predictable limits so God finds it easy to work with. You know what you can do and you know what you can't. You know when you need help. You

SELF-RESPECT: THE SOLUTION TO UNSOLVABLE PROBLEMS

do better and your confidence grows. You feel good about yourself. Respect yourself for loving who you are. Be proud of yourself for wanting to be a better person. Whether you know it or not, it's everyone's goal.

You have to want it. Once you get past your disappointments it's just a matter of applying yourself. Like building a house, you take it step by step; assessing what you need and then you do it. You have to decide what you're willing to pay. You assign everything a priority. You pace yourself. Be wise with your resources. You're always evaluating where you are and how you can do better. You want success but you can enjoy yourself along the way. You don't have to wait to die to know you had a good life. Believe in yourself. You have to find your own solution. Each person's plan brings more Love to life. That's why there's so much variety in human beings. Personalities are different to fit each individual's desires. You appreciate the "custom" work that makes your life your own. You don't have to like everyone. Just know they love themselves, and they believe it's worth what they do to be who they are.

Some people don't care what you want. They only care about themselves. It's how they sustain an image of their self-worth. They don't see you as an equal unless it helps them. When you believe in your opinion you have self-respect. People who want you to believe something other than your self-respect want to control you. They want you to respect them before you respect yourself. When they can't convince you with facts, they'll lean on your emotions to override your common sense. It doesn't matter if it's right for you. They want you to believe what's good for them is what's right for you. But it's always your decision. Anyone who cares about you wants you to respect yourself. They won't deny you something if it costs you your self-respect. You're the only one who knows your priorities. If a salesperson convinces you to buy a sports car for your family of five they're happy to make the commission. Driving a sports car is fun but life isn't all weekend drives up the coast. There are plenty of errands during the week and for that you need a bigger car.

People will sell you anything that makes them money. It's not selfishness. It's trade and everyone has bills to pay. To be fair you must constantly evaluate your intentions. Your goal is to do well in the way *you* define it. Your responsibility is you must define it. Believing in yourself means trusting your ability when you're unsure of the future. It trusts your desire when you don't really know what you want. It trusts your path without letting doubts deter you. It may be hard and you feel you're not ready. Trust what your self-respect tells you. You support yourself by loving yourself.

"Believe in yourself." It's easy to say but what if you don't believe in yourself? What if what you believe is wrong? What if you don't trust yourself? For me, it's anything mechanical. I find it hard to understand mechanical concepts. Some people accept something should work and when it doesn't they fix it. They immediately see the way it works. I have to do something over and over before I trust myself doing it, and if something unusual happens I'm back to square one. I have too many ideas on how things could work instead of focusing on the way that does. I believe in myself for what I'm good at and trust others to do what I can't. Believing in yourself is respecting who you are, not believing you're a super hero. Be a super hero in your *desire* to do the right thing. The process is simple. You answer the first question then you go on to the next.

Beyond the misery is your desire to succeed. You won't be good at everything but you should excel at doing your best. The difference between trying your best and abandoning hope is the measure of your self-respect. You can fail, but as long as you do your best there's nothing to regret. It'll take many failures before you're the person you want to be. You have to smooth out the edges. That's normal for everyone who wants to be a good person. You accept yourself for your maturity and your intention to do well. Then you make the effort. It's your responsibility so it's your decision. Sometimes it's the extra time you spend studying for a career and sometimes it's denying yourself play time while you work two jobs to save money for a house. You appreciate your commitment and respect yourself for it. You learn self-gratitude because you have yourself to thank.

Your self-respect knows life is hard. It takes hard work and luck to succeed. Sometimes you get the job because you know the right person. Sometimes someone else knows the right person and they get the job. It may be unfair but that's human nature. Friends help each other. It's like helping yourself. That's why you should never give up. That's why your goal must serve your soul's purpose, not some transitory ideal. Look beyond the details. Everyone has the same opportunity to make themselves valuable. When you compete for a job, you have to communicate that value to prove you're the right candidate. Everyone's trying to impress people they don't know. Everyone

SELF-RESPECT: THE SOLUTION TO UNSOLVABLE PROBLEMS

wants the power that comes with winning. Add fate and your success may have little to do with you. You might have to wait your turn, but it always comes. Like everyone else, you're entitled to win.

If you don't like waiting then develop a positive attitude because it's likely you'll have to wait. There's nothing wrong with you holding you back. You're just impatient. That's okay. It's normal to want what you want now. You want to feel good NOW! But no one can shower you with fairy dust and make your dreams come true. You may wish you could put a computer chip in your head and know everything, but for now you have to practice and learn. Some days it's your turn and everything works perfectly. Other days life's a burden, like getting the slow cashier at the supermarket. The energy of the day constantly changes. There's no right or wrong. Every day you wake up in a different mood. Every day you need a new skill set to make things work. It's rare to win every time. Your soul doesn't want you to win every time. It grows by overcoming resistance. Nature has demands. "Yesterday was great! Now do it standing on your head." God won't waste an opportunity. It'll explore everything, good and bad. Just know you'll always be rewarded with a new opportunity.

It takes courage to make a decision. You have to trust your judgment. You have to forgive yourself when you make a mistake. Others may be disappointed in you. Life's ups and downs aren't your measure as a person and careless opinions aren't the law. You have a mission to your fate to fulfill. Your job is to make Love part of everything you do. *Love is the measure of your life. It's the love you create; the love you give and the love you receive.* It doesn't identify you by what you own. That's all left behind when you die. Doing something sincerely, even when you fail, carries your hopes through Eternity. That's why people talk about legacies. They want to create value in a future that doesn't exist for them. Today, we're doing so well that shopping's become entertainment. There's less toiling in the fields and none of the uncertainty in hunting game. Now the adventure says, "Buy the new phone!" Today, you can't even get drunk without someone attaching style to it whether it's their knowledge of wines or the right way to talk to the bartender. When so much is style then we must be doing pretty well. You should be grateful for your modern life. Survival is a bitch.

Affectations are often more presentable than character. They're more interesting. They're funnier. It's the sign of a healthy society that doesn't worry about survival. So we have celebrity in the age of social media. Talent isn't needed as long as you put on a good show; a silly dance or a funny saying. Then how should you value yourself? Is success being pulled around by the crowd like a cow with a ring in its nose? It can pay well as long as you keep up the act. The truth is you're perfect no matter what you do. You have everything you need to be successful who you are. The job is: respect your values. Every moment is a new opportunity. There's no valid reason for someone to belittle you. We succeed by helping each other. Everyone matters. Like the tech nerds who rule the world today, you have to find your place in society. Once cotton was king, then steel, then oil, today it's technology. Tomorrow it'll be something else. The world doesn't change. You mature.

Accept yourself and you can play the game the way you want. Don't waste your time cursing fate. Everyone has to adapt. It's part of the game. Everyone asks the same question, "What's the best way to get along with people?" It takes effort *not* to love people. It conflicts with your Nature. "I'll love this one but I won't love that one." It doesn't work that way. It's all one thing. You have to love everyone and not look for an excuse to ignore someone. It's natural to respect yourself but we're in this together. The question is, "Where do you draw the line?" How can you trust someone who's hurt you before? Would you risk your reputation on someone you didn't know? It's a skill not to make a mess of it. Nature can be unpredictable so we depend on each other. There's a rightful place for you or you wouldn't be here. That's the beginning. Find the people who share your hopes. God gave you the ability to dream, so believe in your dreams and do the work.

You're not here to please everyone. You have free will so there's always give and take. Alliances are great; a friendship or a marriage, even a job. It makes life easier when you know someone supports you. You don't worry as much. Life's hard enough without making every step into a battle. Know what you want. Get it or move on. You have responsibilities so be responsible. Do what you have to. Accept yourself but don't accept your situation. Everyone's trying to succeed so they can be a better person. That's why people give away their fortunes. Values are tricky. There are so many priorities it can make your

SELF-RESPECT: THE SOLUTION TO UNSOLVABLE PROBLEMS

head spin. It takes time to learn the nuances. You can spend your whole life never dealing with something then suddenly it's in your lap. Maybe you're a senior citizen forced to take care of an infant relative when some tragedy takes the baby's parents. You do your best. That's all that's asked of you. Your self-respect demands your best. The rest is up to fate.

Who decides your fate? You do. How do you know it's right for you? Because you and God planned it together. The question is the way you confront your values. First, accept who you are. Those are the facts. Don't fight with yourself. Life's enough of a battle. Your soul knows the way. It may be a dismal picture but there's nothing wrong with you. There's nothing you can't change, even if it's just your point of view. Your job is to solve the character puzzle you've been assigned. If you do it right then expect it to be challenging. That's the game. Your safe place is with God. God is the way through it even if the world has to stop while you catch your breath, like the way an illness takes you out of circulation for a while. No matter how confused you are, problems aren't judgments. They show you a way to care about yourself. The problem is you can get lost in all the opinions. Your fate reveals a path. It can be an adventure as long as you don't identify with it. Your fate is a roadmap. It only asks that you be brave.

Celebrate who you are. Include your talents and your foibles. Don't deny yourself. Don't blame yourself. Do your best. Reject the inertia of hopelessness. Take the first step even if it takes a year to take your next step. Support your dreams. Enjoy your desires. Join a gym even if you don't go for six months. Participate. Exercise your free will. Success isn't a talent. It's a sacrifice. It's practice. Stay with it. Like driving a racing car, you have to watch the gauges. You have to judge the turns. There's nothing wrong with you that says you can't have everything. There are lots of people worse off than you who beat the odds and won. Think wheelchair basketball. There's always a way. Trust your self-respect. Everything else is a passing concern.

Appreciate your humanity. What you don't know you'll learn. You're born with the essence of life, your soul. The rest is self-taught. In Spirit everything makes sense. Have a positive attitude and life will prove it to you. You create your opportunities. Focus on the answer and your imagination will find it, often by turning your shortcomings into strengths. Creation is there for you. Love is your reality. Build your life on it. You may feel lost but you're always headed in the right direction. Your soul is your compass and you're always headed home.

Chapter 9
You, Your Soul, & I

Self-respect is the answer to every question because every question at its core is a spiritual question. Your life is a glorious experience no matter how mundane it seems. Your character is a spiritual journey equal to the sum of your gifts and handicaps in relation to the experience your life demands. That's why a failure should never hold you back. Your success is in the experience. You serve Creation by practicing your values. There are too many variables to predict how something might turn out...or what it means to your character. From the way you choose fruit at a farm stand to how you value yourself as a juror to determine justice for a stranger, the essence of your decision is spiritual. Loving yourself with respect for others is the first rule of social conduct. It accepts the unity of souls in our common experience. Choosing fruit with a blemish isn't the end of the world. It's the wildness of life's perfection. It perfectly matches its surroundings because it's part of it. It's perfection not order. Your spiritual mandate is to create order from perfection. Love makes humanity perfect. Your consciousness gives it order. Your soul knows its purpose. It accepts God's mandate despite all the work. You're created in God's image but you're not God. You have the gift of God's creativity to design the life you want. You have God's Light and the right to direct it however you like. You have God's Love and the choice to respect it. But you don't have God's judgment. You don't have God's values. You don't know God's purpose. You don't understand Eternity. You don't see the complexity in Creation. You don't see God's fascination with it. You don't see how every detail affects everything else. Even then you may not think it's worth it. What you're meant to know is limited. What's unlimited is the way you translate Love into life. That's what God likes about you.

You're responsible for your self-respect. No one can do it for you. You wouldn't want them to. It's an opportunity to trust yourself. Where you're weak, build yourself up. Be your own best resource. As long as you're trying to do better, respect yourself. Even when you're confused you're not wrong. You want reliable values. You just don't want to screw up. It's the stability you depend on. It's your life. It's your freedom. It's your soul's wisdom. After all the philosophies you still have to define Love on your own terms. Love's all around you. Feel it. Join it. It wants you to trust it. Its peace proves there's a purpose in this chaos. Nature responds to its infinite possibilities. It's God's endless expressions working together for a common purpose. Your job is to align your spiritual perfection with Nature's creative perfection. The proof that you succeeded is your self-respect.

What exactly is Nature? The key to understanding Nature is appreciating it makes sense. It's logical so you can work with it. You can change it and know what to expect. You know you'll get wet when it rains. The roads will be slick and dangerous. But the Universe is smart. It changes to accommodate the rain. You seek shelter. You slow down. You wait till it stops. You trust your judgment because you've experienced it before. Human beings populate the wilderness then get wiped out by a disease. Then everything comes back to where it was and expands beyond its previous limit. Its potential is never diminished. Nature adapts. You learn from its rhythms. You know the tides and the best time to catch fish. You know to stay away when the mosquitos are breeding if you don't want to get bitten. Nature is life. When you respect it you respect yourself. It's designed to help you. You're designed to use it. It's designed without limits to match your imagination. Nature and creativity work together. Life isn't arbitrary. It's custom-made.

From a distance, it's chaotic. Every part affects everything else and you don't know what it'll do till it happens. Every part is random energy until you define it. Nature feeds your imagination. You're the creation of God's imagination. That's why you ask so many questions. God wants to see its limits in an environment that has no limit. Your job is to create limits. Your job is to have experiences. Your job is to have feelings. Your job is to weigh the values and come up with a plan that respects Love. Everything balances on Love. God's consciousness is Love. If your goal is to succeed, then Love must be part of it. Without Love, life's an excuse. Energy is conscious. Life

SELF-RESPECT: THE SOLUTION TO UNSOLVABLE PROBLEMS

is no illusion. Thinking the world isn't conscious is the illusion. Everything is aware. God created the Universe to question itself. Your job is to explore that awareness. You're the interpreter between Love and Creation. That's a lot to respect yourself for.

You can converse with anything. That's why we name things that describe their identities like *Death Valley* or *The Enterprise*. It's how you interact with the monolithic world. You relate to the individual identity of things. God's Love makes everything equal. Your individuality is a concurrent expression of God's universality. You have a responsibility to God and a responsibility to your identity. Your goal is self-awareness. Your connection to Creation is easy to miss because your focus is caring about yourself. If Creation was stuffed in a bucket, you'd be in that bucket too. No matter how much of an individual you think you are, like you, everything's exploring its existence. The principles of survival are the same. Nourish. Grow. Explore. Create. Evolve. If you want to maintain your identity you have to respect yourself. That's how Nature works. You express your identity or you become part of something else's identity. When you respect yourself, you can be part of many identities.

Your identity is more than your reflection in the mirror. Life has endless identities, each unique to the path it creates. It's a forest and a seed. These are Nature's personalities, like sunny days and hurricanes. They're much like human personalities. You know your own personality when you're honest with yourself. How you align Love with your personality is your life's work. What do you demand? In all the ways energy creates physical form, each form creates the environment it needs to survive. These different "personalities" help God ask more questions. Once something discovers its identity, it can grow on its own and ask the questions God hadn't considered. God wants to see everything evolve; where it came from, where it's going, and how it creates new identities. Why did something evolve the way it did? What values mattered? Curiouser and curiouser, Alice. Your identity is unique because you can change things for no other reason than it's interesting. Like God, you want to see what happens. You want to know what's possible and what you can do with it.

That's God's way. It starts everything on a path then waits to see how it does on its own. That's how God evolves. It's the energy of Creation redone through your creativity. That's your contribution. Creation is God in small pieces. If you want to respect yourself, you have to accept it. You have to trust the equilibrium even when you don't like it because your creativity says you can change it. That's how you respect yourself, loving God by loving Creation. You invest your soul in it. You can live with the pressure because you know it's temporary. How you manage it is your gift to Creation. You're free to do what you like. Life's not meant to frighten you, but there are no time-outs. Even your dreams make demands. There's always something going on asking you to decide. You always have the desire to do better. Life doesn't let up but your self-respect makes it manageable because you know acceptance is your way through the maze.

Respect your identity. It's how you define yourself. You can do anything as long as you follow the rule. The rule protects you. It's the rule to care about each other. It guarantees you'll get your fair share. With so many cultures, the social standard has to respect everyone. That's why we have farm communities, industrial parks, and residential areas. It's how society lets you liberate your identity and still respect your neighbor. You want to make your vison real. You want to feel your power. You have to give your soul an identity whether it's a worn leather jacket or new Gucci shoes. Dress it up. Tune it up. Plan what you'll do with it. Then build your life on it. Your soul doesn't come empty-handed. You have talents. You have dreams. You have the will to succeed. Everyone brings something different. Everyone has a purpose and every purpose matters.

Whoever you think you are, you're an integral part of God's consciousness. You have God's energy. Your free will is God's opportunity. God questions itself in the choices you make. Your values measure your character. It's not easy accommodating Love every time you do something. That's why people find substitutes; things they can buy that make them feel good, things that become a replacement for their soul's success. Your soul needs challenges to prove itself. The material world is easier. You can add things up. If you're the best looking or best dressed, if you have the biggest house or newest car, if you have an attractive personality or know the right people, it's easy think you're successful. The opposite is true too. Without those things it's easy to think you're a failure. Being successful is fine as long as you understand your soul's success is measured by the Love you create, not how shiny you make it.

SELF-RESPECT: THE SOLUTION TO UNSOLVABLE PROBLEMS

Through you your soul meets the Universe. Then you decide what you'll do with it. You might own ten cars but you can only drive one at a time. You can put them together and stare at them but to really enjoy them you have to step on the gas. You have to experience it. Having the most isn't winning. It's an easy way to define winning when you don't understand Love. Your soul doesn't care how much money you have. It cares how you value it. Your soul wants you to have the world as long as it's balanced by Love. Your soul's identity is Love. If you want the world to matter then measure it by Love. And you have to decide what it means when you're not exactly sure how it works. It's okay to care about yourself first. It's okay to make mistakes. But you're bound by your existence to be a loving person. When you do, everything fits. When you don't, you may be successful but you won't be happy. You still need God's blessing, and for that you need Love.

Your soul is your true identity. It existed before you were born. It's your eternal nature, your predilections and talents. It's the environment you're drawn to. It's why you're fascinated by some things and bored by others. Your soul is unique because it sees everything in light of your experience. It depends on your intuition to connect with your nature. Life's demanding. You may have more compelling interests than what you're doing now. Free will gives you the right to change. What makes you unique isn't an accident. Your soul knows what it wants. Your soul has a plan. Then you're born and everything's a muddle. In Spirit everything made sense. But life is unpredictable so it's wise to question it. Your identity is your response to life. In a way it's no more exotic than a child's puzzle. From the mess of pieces you have to match the picture. It's not perfect. There's no "perfect" other than what you're willing to accept. Every soul is already perfect when it asks God, "Who am I?" You're perfect when you respect your values. Like mastering a tricky dance step, it's fun when you get it right.

Everything has an identity. Like an artist's style, it's the image they create and how they communicate it. Their art is a refinement of all the energy they've ever known. Their personality is in their style. Every business has an identity whether it's a Silicon Valley start-up or a multi generation family pizzeria. Communities have identities as towns and neighborhoods. Nature has identities in the variety of life. The point is life is not a mish-mash. It didn't evolve these identities by chance. God conceptualized them as opportunities to ask questions. Everything makes sense. Every expression of Nature has something to say about itself. Everything interacts. Individual identities combine to create more intricate identities like jungles with so many identities it's impossible to define anything. And we cheer when we find a new species. As a human being your talent is to see the identity in a tree and use it to create the identity of a house. Your soul is the mechanism God uses in the same way you use a lure to catch a fish. It's attractive. Every lure is different for the best chance to catch a kind of fish. And it's the same for every identity.

Creation is your medium. It's the substance of your art. Your art is your identity... and your reality. You create your identity then raise your kids to create their identities. Hopefully, it's centered on Love but those are the choices you have to make. God created Nature's identities and it's up to you to use them the best you can. So the developer takes the identity of a lake and builds a hotel there so guests can enjoy swimming and boating. They create the identity of a resort. When noisy boaters disturb the peaceful picnickers, it's a matter of setting limits so everyone can enjoy the lake in their own way. That's civilization. Whole generations have identities like "Baby Boomers" and "Millennials." It's endless. You create the concepts that become your identity and it's often as simple as how you wear your hat. Love measures everything. Love is the essence of every identity. Whatever you create, Love gives it value. Love is Creation's identity.

Love respects your identity. It respects your responsibility to it. It's how you fit God's plan. It's your purpose. It's how you respect yourself for your contribution to Creation. It's a revelation. It feels good. You're the product of every step the world takes. Your future is in its next step. You're defined by your identity. Every problem has a goal that can't be reached any other way. Your purpose is your soul's dream and hope for a good life. There's wisdom in your aspirations. It's Love building the bridges you'll need for the future.

Everything is part of something else. You know how atoms form the elements that Nature molds into beetles and bananas. Then along comes human beings and transforms those creations into things that make our lives better, like zoos and banana cream pie. Your creativity wants satisfaction. It wants to be useful. Your will focuses your imagination. That's how you create God's experiences. Creation is God's identity. God's growth comes from human

SELF-RESPECT: THE SOLUTION TO UNSOLVABLE PROBLEMS

beings questioning Creation. That's how God explores itself. Love tests life any way it can. But you don't have to force every door. There are plenty of doors open to you. You can enjoy the identity of every living soul plus the unique identity you create for yourself. God created Nature but you give it meaning. You give it its purpose. Respect yourself for that. Love what you're doing. You can deny your self-respect but you can't avoid it. It's an unbearable feeling when you don't respect yourself. That's why God always stays close.

Everything has an identity. It's the independence God gave Nature so every part could evolve in its own way. It makes you ask, "Why this way? Why not that way?" That's what God asks. When you respect yourself you open to God's possibilities. Your gift is you have the ability to reinterpret Nature. You have the power of Creation in your will. Your only limit is you must abide by Love. Then you can process your desires into any reality you want. God will help you. It's not a secret. You honor God in your respect for your identity. When you respect Love you become the creative force God meant you to be. Respect the Universal Consciousness. It's God asking, "How do you create a personality for yourself that respects everything?" It's really not a test for you. You're a volunteer. It's a test for God.

You have to work on your social skills. You have to cooperate with Nature. You learn to compromise. It doesn't mean giving in every time. You still want a fair deal. That's the work of it. Nature doesn't change much and when it does it goes slowly. Human beings are the engines of change. As soon as they think of something they want it. It means you have to keep up. You may not know everything but you can question it. That's being smart. Intelligence is what you know, how fast you can get to it, and how you accommodate new information. How you apply it is your creativity. Accept Nature's identities. It could be a bored clerk or a hot summer day. As one thought, Creation loves everything. But in life each part competes for survival. When you see a car accident you stop to help, but when you're forced to merge into traffic you jockey for every inch so you don't lose your turn. These are the compromises you make every day. It's how you coordinate mutual respect. At the same time you have to respect yourself to be sure you get your fair share.

You created your identity. It's your response to life. It's your personality. It's the values you chose to support your consciousness. It's your being; your body, mind, feelings, culture, finances, and general opinion of life. It's not your vison. Your vision is your creative freedom. You create your vision in the way you manage your priorities. It's your spiritual purpose, your reaction to your fate. Respect your opportunities then live your life. Get advice from others. How do they see their life? There's support in opinions, just don't follow every idea over a cliff. It's got to feel right to you. While you may not be perfectly positioned, your soul accepts this. You have a purpose in Creation. It doesn't make sense to have every life be the same when there are so many opportunities in our differences. An orchestra can play many types of music while a ukulele, no matter how good the player is, always sounds like a ukulele.

Every soul has an identity. That identity pushes you to play tennis with your friends or be alone to practice the guitar. You can do either, neither, or both. Your soul's inclinations are the basis for your personality. Your personality is your plan for life. In a way, it foretells the future. It guides your maturity. Your maturity is measured by how well you include Love in your life. You may have an expressive personality so being an exhibitionist gets you the attention you want. You find comfort in that part of your personality. You might have a reserved personality so you create a reticent persona to avoid anything that requires too much negotiation. You create a simple life and you like it that way. Your soul looks for the best way to express itself. Fortunately, you have God's help. Unfortunately, you probably don't trust it. God is there for you whether you acknowledge it or not. But if you have faith, you'll find you're both pulling in the same direction.

Maybe you don't believe in God. Giving up your free will to a conceptual identity might not work for you no matter how attractive it is. You may have a logical mind that demands proof. The truth is you believe in thousands of things just because you heard it somewhere. So why not believe me? Trust your self-respect. You want to be sure something's relevant then decide for yourself. The same way you want your account balance from the bank, you want proof from your faith that what you believe is true. The problem is faith's proofs are mostly anecdotal. Miracles are great, but then you have to believe in miracles. Maybe it's just hard work or good luck. The way people prove God is by trusting their experience. If you trust the person telling you about God then it's worth it to see if it can happen to you. Don't be concerned you might fail. You'll never incur God's wrath when you try

SELF-RESPECT: THE SOLUTION TO UNSOLVABLE PROBLEMS

to do the right thing. God shares your hopes. Many people claim positive experiences so it's worth exploring. Miracles are real and there's a part of you that feels it. It means you have another good reason to respect yourself.

God will never ignore you, even when you feel you're alone. In return, God asks for your attention. You don't need a thousand years of history to justify your belief. God only asks that you question the possibility that God is real. You control less than you think and never the result. A result can take you anywhere. God's plan balances on knowing there's a positive aspect to every relationship. From your point of view, you want a benefit. You want to know your purpose so you can help it along. You want to know your responsibilities so you can make better choices. You want clear values. You want to feel good. Great! God will show you everything. You respect God through your free will. God wants to know your interpretation of *conscious awareness*. It's God's never-ending question for itself, "What am I?" Feeling good sends you in the right direction. Good and bad exist to give you a choice. Life's a multiple choice test with only two answers that keep repeating themselves: yes or no. Don't judge yourself when things don't work out. Respect your ability to create an alternative and keep trying. Love yourself. Time empowers every plan and you never know how much you'll need.

You can do anything. Wherever you focus your attention you'll succeed. Some doors are open and you stumble right through them. Other doors are shut and you can't budge them no matter what you do. Make your life easier. Use your common sense. Go where life leads you. It doesn't matter how long it takes. You may never be the star quarterback or prima ballerina. There's too much competition and few opportunities. Part of your job is to create more opportunities. Any interest beyond your survival is worthy of respect. Whatever you think deserves a second look energizes God. It's your interest in Creation. It's how you express God's purpose. "Why is it like that?" You ask because that's what God asks. Respecting yourself respects God. It's not your respect for religious dogma but it can be. Dogma has its place if you respect it. You create a vision to match your identity. The only rule is: Love must be part of it. God's consciousness is Love. Love guides Creation's energy. It's not an afterthought. Love won't satisfy everyone but it satisfies God.

God helped create your identity. Now God helps you on your way. God knows your problems. God uses them to teach you more about Love. Your identity helps you answer life's question, "What am I supposed to do?" You hope for guidance, but you may have to wait while your maturity catches up so you can guide yourself. Your identity helps you make the choices that support your decisions. You have the intellect. You have the attitude. You have your soul's intention. You have God's Love and Creation's energy. You have everything the Creator has. Build your life on it. You can change your goals. You can change your priorities but you have to trust your values. With God, every question has an answer. Be brave. We all have to work through the details. With Love, everything's connected. The answer to life is in pieces until you put it together. Guide your imagination with Love and your soul will find a way.

God finds you fascinating. You created a personality for yourself. There's a different one for each of us. It could be brand new or an adjustment to something you already know. It's sure to challenge you…and comfort you too. You're special. But your independence may not get you what you want. You probably need help. So adjust your personality to be open to anyone who excels at what you can't do, like a doctor or mechanic. You respect yourself by doing what's in your best interest. It's always in your best interest to be honest with yourself. Trust your sincerity. Trust your plan. You're limited by Nature but not bound by it. That's what your creativity is for. Have faith. It'll help you side-step the maelstrom of half-baked ideas that seem like the easy way out. There's always a best way. Know what you want. Improve on what you have. Change the players. Add harmony. Slow it down. Speed it up. You produce what you aim at. With all its ups and downs, life was custom-made for you. Add a positive attitude and you'll find your self-respect.

Your soul has a plan. Life is the work God requires for it. Love guides it all. Putting Love to work is what your life's about. If it's confusing, ask God for help. You have an unbreakable connection to God. You can call it what you like, but you share its consciousness. You feel it. You feel it in others. It's everywhere. Regardless of the differences, everything knows Love. Love is God's consciousness. Creation is its form. If you want to be complete, you must find peace with its energy. You can see it as individual pieces or all one thing. That's your decision and you can change it anytime. Your life matters

SELF-RESPECT: THE SOLUTION TO UNSOLVABLE PROBLEMS

but you're just one part of it. Still, it has to work for you. Creation wants you to succeed. You know what you want, so ask Creation to give it to you. Life is a balance of mutual responsibilities. You must pay your fair share, but Creation has a debt to you that must be paid as well. For Creation to succeed you must be included.

Bad times can't stop your creativity. Just the opposite, bad times fuel your creativity. You experience life through your mind. It's your judgment about things. It's your values. Your body has limits but your soul is eternal. So pain is temporary and Love is forever. You might invent a medicine that relieves the pain of millions, but you're equally successful saying the words that ease a friend's despair. You don't need the adulation of millions to be successful. You need a good opinion of yourself. You judge your thoughts. Respect God's values and you'll be good at it.

Chapter 10
If you were God, what would you do differently?

You want the best from life. You want it to be fair. You want help when you need it. You want achievable goals. You want to feel good. You want life's balance to favor you. You have an opinion of what life should be. But things don't always work out. It's frustrating because you know you can make it whatever you like. If you respect your creativity and respect life's limits, then you can make your life the same way God made Creation. There's nothing beyond your reach. Just arrange the physics. It's logical and you're supported by Love. You don't have to be God to act like God. You're already the hand of God. You're born with God's ability to manipulate Creation.

Why do you suffer when you can change things? Because life's an exercise. God doesn't know what it is, so you're here to help find out. God wants to understand itself. Where did it come from? What does infinite mean? God wants your help to explore it. Your soul doesn't care how much you weigh. Your soul cares what your body means to you as an expression of Love. Do YOU care about it? Do you respect the opportunities it gives you? You might think there is no God. How could a loving God ignore all the misery in the world? But if there is no God and there is no afterlife, why do people put up with it? What about life is so attractive? Why do you care about people you don't know? Why do you have a sense you want to accomplish something? Why do people rarely give up? They'd rather suffer than die. Look at all the homeless. At the bottom of the barrel they still do their best to survive. If you wake up with a head cold and expect to be sick for a week, why don't you just kill yourself and end your misery now? You can certainly expect more head colds in the future. It's because life is compelling and the opportunity to learn something is even more compelling.

God is real even if you have a hard time believing it. Love is supreme. Love connects everything. Love is God's consciousness. Light is God's energy. They combine in Creation, the spiritual and material, self-aware energy…God. You define its purpose. That's why you have free will. God wants to see what you do with it. That's how God learns. Your soul is wise even when you're confused. It's the eternal nature of Creation that minimizes life's problems in comparison. Life's problems always get solved. You either work through the problem or you go on to the next world and start again. Either way, it's over. But life can be tedious. It's hard to see yourself as a perfect soul. The daily grind is consuming. You have to make decisions as a player, not an observer from some ethereal realm. Failure is a possibility and there's no one to blame. It's on you. That's the problem. Life takes work. It's work to survive and work to respect yourself. If you don't like it, try something else.

You see all the pain in the world. You have your own pain. If God really loved everyone why would it let you suffer? You want to live in your dream house. Why doesn't God give it to you? You'd like a new car, maybe three or four cars. An SUV and a sports car would be nice. And wouldn't you like stylish clothes and a great body to show them off? Don't you want the career of your dreams and maybe even be famous? Everything that's not important, you want. Don't get me wrong. Those are fun distractions and you should have what you want. It's just they don't give you much in return. They give you the illusion of well-being, not the reality. Of course you want to be comfortable but self-respect, good health, a supportive family, and caring friends are your wealth. Love is your wealth. God's reality is Love. It's the creative energy that makes you whole no matter what. Problems are hard teachers. You don't want to endure more than you have to. As much as you may not like the lesson, that's how you learn. The pain may seem unbearable but if God can bear it so can you. Peace is in your faith. Faith is your protection. God knows your limits and trusts you as a partner. God has faith in you.

You're an eternal soul. When you're growing up, a year seems like a long time to wait to get your driver's license. Maybe it's four years to graduate college. It could be a lifetime disability, but eventually the waiting ends. Your

SELF-RESPECT: THE SOLUTION TO UNSOLVABLE PROBLEMS

turn comes up. Eternity has time for everything. You'll never miss anything because you don't have the time. Life's schedules are predetermined. Like a butterfly's metamorphosis, it takes the time in stride. Peace of mind tells you to accept it because there's nothing you can do. Patience makes sense but your free will may not agree. Life's a long day with a beginning, an end, and no guarantee. You want to enjoy every minute. You don't want it too boring or too rough. Like *Goldilocks*, you want it "just right." But your idea of perfect may not fit God's purpose. God asks questions and, for you, that means problems.

They won't be fun problems either, like deciding which shirt to wear. God will challenge you. God doesn't care how hard it is because it can end it in an instant. God can solve your problem today or let you suffer till the day you die. God doesn't want you to suffer. God wants you to ask questions. God wants you to compare values. Many people do their best and still struggle. A simple prayer may be all they need. "God, please help me." It's not complicated. It's an easy way to tell God that you've had enough and you don't know what else to do. It can often stop a problem immediately. You've done all you can. God won't let you suffer for no reason. God loves you too much There has to be a benefit. Love must be its meaning. There's no in-between. God will support you regardless of the path you choose. Love is your direction. Find harmony with it. Every pain passes. That's God's promise. You'll never fail at life. The experience is your success.

Life's measure is the Love you create. It's not how well you survive. No matter who you are you can't survive a disaster. A disaster takes everyone. It could be a tidal wave or a plane crash, but there's nothing you can do. You can't dig a hole so deep that you can hide from a genetic disposition to a heart attack. God will give you the right problem. Respect it so you can avoid what's unnecessary. Your common sense weighs the risk. That's how you respect yourself in harmony with God's purpose. It's the benefit of a long life. There are more opportunities to evaluate your maturity. You can only control yourself so work on your character. Be honest and caring. Learn when to be patient and when to stand your ground. Caring doesn't mean sacrificing yourself. It means respecting Love. Caring is the job of questioning fairness. It's a skill you have to learn. Every identity has a place in Creation. Your respect for yourself is your courage to be who you are.

Why does God tolerate a lack of Love in the world? Because there is no lack of Love. It's everywhere. But it's confusing. It's meant to be. You're meant to question it. You're meant to clarify it. You might ask God, "Why isn't life easier?" It's because life's challenges express values that can't be achieved any other way. Challenges create choices that reveal faith's support. If everything was easy, what's the point, to have more stuff? You're an eternal being. You already have Creation. If you were too comfortable you'd miss the joy in achieving your goal. Having this year's model is a small reward. Without a struggle there's no need for compassion. Compassion shares the burden. The weird thing is it needs suffering to exist. Compassion creates Love but suffering sets the stage. God created pain to show you Love can heal it. God created tough problems to prove, no matter what, Love always wins. As attractive as a "perfect" world seems, problems are where Love shines.

Hardship is one thing but the misery some people suffer seems senseless. Why should someone live as an invalid depending on others for survival? Why should a child spend their short life in a hospital bed never to reach their 10th birthday? How could God be so cruel when it could end it all in a thought? God isn't cruel. One way or another life's tragedies end. You may want a life without problems but that wouldn't satisfy your soul. Your soul's job is to find balance so it needs imbalance to work with. There's always a trade-off. A big house means more rooms to clean. You can hire someone but then you have to live with a stranger. Remember Isaac Newton, "For every action there's an equal and opposite reaction." It's the same for consciousness. Life is full of questions and you need Love to answer them. Years after you made a bad decision you'll still have regrets. It's Love reminding you, you can be a better person. It's your respect for Love that proves, spiritually, you know what you're doing. God loves you for pushing yourself. While winning is different for everyone, the Love of winning is the same.

You cooperate or you compete; whether it's business or national pride. Cooperation means everyone wins. Competition means winners and losers. Do you have to win? Do you have to stand out? Does winning make you a better person? You compete because it creates opportunities for everyone. Cooperation creates different opportunities. You can shoot baskets by yourself or find someone to play with for some one-on-one. Together you make it a game. Instead of a fantasy, you make it real. Now it can test you.

SELF-RESPECT: THE SOLUTION TO UNSOLVABLE PROBLEMS

Taken to extremes it can be a national obsession like the World Cup. You form teams and the teams create energy. They create enthusiasm. They create pressure. Then you direct the pressure. Life's a game. It has goals and rules. It has expectations. Like sports, it has quarters and innings, college and pros, Little League, logos, and the hall of fame. Everyone competes because life demands personal responsibility. Everyone has to eat. Life is your Olympics and once you're here you have to play. Remember, whatever happens, Love is going to win. When you respect Love, then you win.

Competition forces you to do better if you want to win. It hurts to lose. It feels bad. Winners feel the exhilaration of success. Losers feel lousy. Losing at anything can make you think you're a bad person, that you don't deserve your own self-respect. The only thing losing should teach you is you want to be a winner. You have to know the difference to avoid misjudging yourself. As a soul, and this goes for every soul, you're perfect. By your spiritual nature you're already a winner. Your purpose is to have experiences and you can do that in your sleep. As a human being, anything can happen and that includes terrible mistakes or extraordinary achievements. God sees your soul. God measures your life by the Love you create; the Love you give and the Love you receive. Your life has no particular result that makes it a success. Your soul's success is in the experience. It doesn't matter what that experience is. It only matters that Love guides your choice at the moment of decision. Whatever the conflict is, ask yourself, "What's Love's role here?" Then you're thinking like God. Like a child playing blocks, you do one thing then take it apart and do something else. You don't worry if a piece falls off. It's the same for an adult. Whatever happens, let your emotions run their course then start again.

You wouldn't want to end competition just because losing makes you feel bad. Losing should make you want to do better. In careers like sports and acting, personal performance is so important that competitors form affection for each other. They know the sacrifice it takes to succeed. They know the effort it takes to make the team or get a part when there are other qualified people with the same goal. There are limited opportunities. They reach a level of excellence where success can mean a different winner every day. Some things you can't control. You might sprain your ankle on the morning of the big game or suffer a casting director having a bad day. It's part of competition.

You can't make yourself so perfect that life won't find a way for you to lose or, really, give your opportunity to someone else. Anyone who works hard is entitled to win even if it means losing sometimes. You'll get your fair share. Winning has to fit your soul's purpose. It doesn't mean you give any less effort. It means you keep trying because it keeps you in the game. Before you can win, you need the opportunity to win.

Competition defines life. Success competes with failure. Life competes with death. Love keeps it all together and gives it direction. It trusts every part will do its best. Every moment changes your priorities. You keep asking, "What's best now?" It's how you value Love. Nothing exists without Love. You can acknowledge it or not. Like a game of poker, life keeps repeating itself. One hand you win, the next hand it's someone else even though you want to win every time. The cards are shuffled and you start again. Regardless of the cards, you respect yourself as a human being. You enjoy winning as part of the game, not that you're better than anyone else. It's a game. Everyone wants to win. The point of the game is to beat the odds with a little mystery thrown in. It's not the money. You can pitch pennies for a thousand dollars a throw. Bluffing depends on the competition. You're not going to bluff a straight flush out of the game no matter what you have, but sometimes you have to try.

So God creeps into your poker night. Poker is about choices and God loves when you have to make choices. Win or lose doesn't matter. God wants to see how your values compete. Do you have the self-respect to love yourself when your life is at stake, like choosing a mate or a career? That's what life's about. You may not want to play. You may not like the risk. It's meant to be hard but you're not meant to suffer. Creation supports you. You're part of it. You benefit from it. In a way, you're competing against yourself. Win or lose, you build your life. Rest and recover but don't give up. There's always a way to win. Give yourself time. Respecting God means respecting your opportunities, not winning every time. That would take the fun out of life even if it means laughing about it later. Success is self-respect at peace with a problem. Self-respect is always at peace.

Tension builds strength but it has to be appropriate. It's a costly use of your energy. It takes a commitment so it has to be controlled. It has advantages but it can be exhausting. It needs time to organize itself even when you like what

SELF-RESPECT: THE SOLUTION TO UNSOLVABLE PROBLEMS

you're doing. Power isn't always physical strength. You don't need muscles to make a speech. You need a good sense of communication. You figure if you hit the right notes good fortune will follow. That's the traditional idea of success; work hard and have a positive attitude. In the absence of a short cut it makes sense. But life takes courage because failure is always a possibility. No matter what your advantages, nothing's guaranteed. You would think God, an entity that can do whatever it wants, should be your guarantee. You'd be right. So if God is real, then life's turmoil must have a purpose. But if everything in Heaven is perfect, why would God create imperfection? God must see a benefit in it. Life's really not imperfect. It's conflicted. If Heaven is perfection seeking to understand itself then life is chaos trying to realign itself. So God approaches the question from both sides. God recreates perfection by taking things apart and then putting them back together in new ways. The tool God uses is you. The glue God uses is Love.

You may not want to play. Life can be hard. Whether you know it or not you do want to play because that's what you're here for. For this you have God's Love. Your problems have a limited duration even if it's every day for the rest of your life. While you measure yourself by your welfare, God measures you by the Love you create. Love, God's consciousness, and Light, God's energy, are God's physical being in the same way your body and soul are your physical being. That's why self-respect is important. It recognizes you as a creative force, an independent expression of God's Love. Life's details have no eternal purpose. Success and failure are learning experiences. Feeding yourself is important. A recipe is a game. Games have their place. They make life's mysteries interesting. The question is how you value them. That value shouldn't exceed your respect for Creation. You're like God but you're not God. You won't get it right every time. What's important is asking the right question every time. The perfect answer can take years to find, because you often have to ask the same question many times before you understand it.

Why does God make you suffer? Why are you so often at odds with God? Isn't there a better way? If you can't have everything just by wishing for it, what's the point of free will? What does "free will" mean if you're limited by Nature? Shouldn't it all be easier? Shouldn't you win every time? Shouldn't you always be happy? You want good things for yourself. You want good things for everyone. You may not jump for joy when a competitor does well but you share your pride in humanity when some sports star breaks a record. And you commiserate with anyone suffering misfortune. No matter how competitive you are, there's a place in your heart that knows you're part of Creation. Life develops your character. Self-respect is its fulfillment. Your problems have a useful purpose. You just have to see it that way.

How could you make God better? You'd probably want an easier life. You'd want less suffering. You'd want more victories. That's the conundrum of a perfect soul. You're already where you want to be, but once you're born you lose sight of your perfection. Life has its own demands. The threats are more immediate. They're more confusing. Values and opinions get jumbled together. Your experience isn't supposed to be all bliss neither should it be discarded as an illusion. Life puts your soul to work. With the endless dynamics of life's tribulations you're meant to recreate God's harmony. If you removed the problems, you'd eliminate the opportunities too. For God, the problem *is* the solution. It just needs an answer. God always asks, "How will Love make this work?" Your soul's mandate is to make your effort and God's purpose work together.

You can do whatever you like. Free will is yours so *you can imagine a better life any way you want*. It's not having the "bling." It's not having people envy you. It's making Love your priority no matter what your circumstance. It's enjoying the courage of an open mind and trusting God's plan. God won't abandon you. God has compassion for you. Life may seem hopeless, but your troubles are minor compared to the misery of being in prison or suffering an incurable disease. After all, God created the horrors that condemn so many to hopelessness. The answer is you *can* do something. You can stand up to God. You can make your case that those hardships should end and more souls should have a better life. Put Love first. Translating Love into reality means prioritizing it. Then you can enter life's contest with God by your side.

Being "too easy" is another challenge. The question becomes, "How can you be productive when you already have more than you need?" How do you respect your time when you have so much? Abundance is a responsibility. Distractions are attractive but you don't learn that much. Lessons are easy to ignore when they don't seem necessary. Your purpose defines you. Your identity focuses on your purpose. There are many ways to do the same thing, all with different benefits. Think, "Making a living." Don't dream about

SELF-RESPECT: THE SOLUTION TO UNSOLVABLE PROBLEMS

doing nothing. Find a worthwhile challenge. Make your soul work for you. It wants to. You're designed to explore your life till the day you die. Enjoy your maturity. Enjoy your confidence. Use your experience. You've earned it. It deserves respect. Honor your self-respect by doing things; whether it's building a faster spaceship or wiping a tear from a child's eye. Life is your education. It's God's evolution. God's purpose is to question its existence from every point of view because there is no final answer. There are only the infinite possibilities in Creation. That's the point. You risk failure every day so God can succeed.

Managing your life is relatively easy. Managing someone else's life is near impossible. Everyone has free will and the responsibility to use it. But you must control it. You need tolerance to accommodate it. You communicate your limits through your emotions. You exercise your self-respect in how you value your relationships. How much of yourself are you willing to invest? You can't force an emotional bargain. You must cooperate. There's a good chance you'll get it right when you respect everyone's limits. Then everyone gets what they want. Emotions have to be handled like a fragile, glass bowl. They can be dependable for years then shatter under the pressure of illness, financial problems, or any of the stresses life forces you to endure to the breaking point. The questions become, "How do you maintain a positive attitude when your life is falling apart? How do you protect your stability when your emotions are out of control? How do you protect your security when you feel weak and ineffective?" The answer always starts, "Slow down." Emotions present immediate questions while your mind needs time to prepare the right answer.

Don't impose yourself on anyone. Reasonable people have reasonable values. Your feelings guide you. They keep your morals intact. When it comes to yourself, it's okay to be demanding. You want moral values that align with your self-respect. You expect the Universe to be fair. Rightfully so. Without a clear sense of right and wrong you're likely to fantasize your feelings. That can lead to fooling yourself; believing in relationships that aren't real. When you're confronted by the truth, you're either honest with yourself and accept the challenge or you give up and suffer the predicament. Either way, you need help. The status quo has been tipped. You must regain your balance. Defusing a conflict is part of getting along with people. Ask yourself, "Where's the limit of tolerance you'll accept?" Much of what you think is important is a convenience with no lasting effect. Fighting over feelings has no purpose other than reinforcing the illusion of loneliness. Unity is your nature. Peace is your rightful place. It's not dependent on anyone else unless you make it dependent. Have hope. Hope tells you good people will find a fair compromise.

People can be frustrating. "Why doesn't everyone think the same way you do? Why are they so confused? Why are they so contrary?" Because it's their responsibility, failure is real, and it's easy to get lost thinking about problems. But it's often wasted energy on non-existent problems. The thought may not be logical. Then you wind up juggling the stress and hating it. Negative thoughts represent problems so you have to respect them. A negative thought can become a bad habit. Instead of disappearing into the wispy world of castoff ideas, they become real. Then you have to clean it up. You have the work of getting back to the original thought so you can change it. A positive attitude means you're always working on your thoughts. Positive thoughts eliminate negative thoughts. They're important because they create your reality. It's as simple as that. You only have room for one thought at a time. If it's negative, stop thinking it. Replace it with a positive thought. Look at life for the benefits. Be sincere. Assign everything a value then handicap the possibilities and place your bet. If the possibilities are real, then trust your fate. You've done everything you could.

Define yourself as a positive person. Self-respect justifies a good opinion of yourself. It joins you to Creation. You meet life together. You mature and come to understand how it works. Nature creates resistance. Then you have to find the silver lining that makes it worthwhile. Don't own your problems. Own the benefits in them. You have a psychic immune system...Love. It protects you from non-existent failures. Most problems don't matter. Like getting stuck in traffic, negative feelings energize the disappointment and make it worse, i.e. "road rage." You live in your thoughts so be happy. Don't make problems. Let your problems find you.

What does God want? Where did God come from? It started with energy... then the miracle. The energy became self-aware. It became conscious. It became God. But it couldn't define itself. It was all energy. So it expressed an intention. It wouldn't just be conscious energy. It would split into two.

SELF-RESPECT: THE SOLUTION TO UNSOLVABLE PROBLEMS

The energy became Light which became thought which became the material Universe we call Creation. Consciousness became Love which became spirituality which expressed as emotion to explain how Creation's connected. So God created the Universe we know today, thoughts and feelings. Now God could experiment. Your job is to have values and make choices. It's your free will. God gave you freedom to see what you'd do with it. God loves new things. That's why we twerk today instead of doing the mambo. God knows it can never answer the question where the energy came from. But when it comes to Creation, God knows everything.

You want to feel good. You want to be comfortable. Comfort is sympathetic. There's support in sympathy. It wants your needs satisfied. It knows Love supports everything. Recognizing consciousness in inanimate things can be a stretch. Most people think consciousness is making choices and doing things. They don't see Nature having a choice. They see it locked in pre-determined patterns. They don't see atomic particles having a choice. But they do. You don't have to be psychic to feel Creation. You're naturally aware. It's what aboriginal cultures did before everyone got so smart. Sometimes the world doesn't include you. It's not against you. It's just the pieces aren't ready to fit. You still need help so you have sympathy for yourself. But sympathy means sharing your feelings. If the only sympathy you can find is yourself, then your only hope is God. Competition can push you aside but you can always depend on God. It's literally everywhere. It's unsettling because you have to give up your self-control, your trust in yourself. It's uncomfortable in the beginning but the angels will show you how.

God enjoys Creation. It likes changing things to see what happens. That's why your worst problem isn't as bad as it seems. It's life in its natural state recycling itself. It'll repeat itself tomorrow or in a hundred years. Social consciousness has limited variations so it needs a solid background for your imagination. There's always an end and there's always the potential to teach you something. God sees everything. Each of us is unique. Your contribution is to explore life from your perspective. Your choices help define God's destiny. Most of it doesn't matter. The Love in your choices matters. Still, you want it to be as easy as possible. You want your hopes to be real. It's the fun part of buying a lottery ticket. You can have whatever you want right now. Love is the Universe in harmony with itself so pay attention to the little things. When you create something, it affects everything. You just have to be patient and not give up.

You're probably not interested in taking risks so God does it for you. Life is a big risk. It can kill you. Or it could mean barely escaping a terrible accident. Your soul wouldn't create those terrors without a good reason. It's not intellectualizing a fantasy. These are life-changing experiences. They force you to pay attention. They make you consider the value of life and how to do better. You can create like God but can you love like God? God wants you to understand this because God's reality is Love. Love is God's consciousness. Your problems don't deserve the importance you give them. Mortality is the end for everyone. Don't ignore your potential because it takes work. Your success isn't yours to judge. Life is about complex values and seeing a positive side to your disappointments. Accept everything. It's easy to say and hard to do. But that's life. There's no right or wrong. There's only your desire to be a loving person. It's not easy for anyone. But when you respect the process, you respect yourself.

Chapter 11
Motivation

Life is compelling. You're born and you immediately have needs. Without even thinking, you're drawn to your comfort. You cried when you were hungry. You cried to go to sleep. You cried to be changed. You cried to be held. Innately you knew what mattered. While everyone has needs, different things are more important to each of us. It makes life personal. Personal means life reacts to your choices in the way you want. The results become your values so you can repeat the ones you like. You want comfort: You want to be dry. You want to be fed. You want to be clean. You want to be engaged. You want to know how. You want to be loved. You want to feel Love. You want Peace. And you want to be sure about it. You endure all life's hungers. You have to. It's the only way there is. Once you're here you have to respect it, and you have to work with it.

Beauty is Love in its physical form. That's why you want to be with it, whether it's an inspiring painting or a charismatic personality. They're attractive because Love is attractive. Beauty is a perception. You learn early on, "Beauty is in the eyes of the beholder." Some people like angel tattoos and others want fiery skulls. Beauty isn't a specific ideal. It's misinterpreted because it's easier to understand beauty as the epitome of perfection. The epitome of perfection is Love. So it's everywhere in everything. It's a rose's bloom or a successful business. It's the perfect angle in an artist's sketch. It's a shout for joy or a dissertation on poverty. It's personal to match your perception of it. Your interpretation is your life's work. It sees beauty in a way that fits you. You identify Love by accepting the beauty in things. It's more than a physical presence. It's the Love it represents. It's not having a perfect nose. A healthy breath is a perfect nose. Every culture has its own perception of beauty and it all revolves around free will. It evolves to match who you are. That's why it's fun to see old fashions…and especially to see tomorrow's fashions. The common thread is it includes your imagination. Life's the same for everyone. Figuring it out your own way is what makes it beautiful.

Beauty is the great motivator. You always want beauty in your life. It's a new car or a good joke. It's a fortunate turn of events or the first day of spring. You're attracted to it even if it's a moment's glimpse out an airplane window. It's success. You want it. You feel it. It recognizes God's handiwork. It's the idea that fits the moment. It's feeling your strength come back after an injury or graduating college. It's a great success or even a good try. But it's only a perception of reality because it separates God into pieces. Different things are beautiful to different people for different reasons at different times. Every interpretation is valid. Every point of view should be respected. An ugly weed can be the miracle ingredient in a new medicine. Even the worst of our natures can be beautiful, like a well-designed prison. Beauty is the perfect answer to the perfect question. You and God can make anything beautiful. You just have to see it in the right light. Like John Keats wrote, "A thing of beauty is a joy forever." It doesn't mean from this moment on it's beautiful. It means it's always been beautiful. You just had to see it that way.

Self-respect is beautiful. It's like having your own lighthouse. It sends a beacon out to the world. It signals, "Love is here." Like a magic charm, your sincerity focuses the Universe. It promises hope. That's your motivation. It's your unification with Love. It's your recognition of the beauty in yourself. It's your power to join with God and change the world in the way you want. Love is Creation's consciousness. It wants you to trust it. It wants you to trust your satisfaction with it. You have a place in Creation. Somehow you'll succeed. Your free will gives you unlimited opportunities. Life can't stop you. It's only a guide. Decide what you want. Be open to it in ways you hadn't planned. Life's an adventure. As long as you're happy, nothing else matters. With Creation, you already have everything. Combining it in new ways is what your free will is for. You direct its energy. That's your power. Love it and you'll always do the right thing. If there are a thousand things you first have to do first, you'll do them. And you'll do them easily because it's who you are. Accept your fate then go on from there.

Motivation meets self-respect in your priorities. Everyone wants the perfect answer… just on their own terms. So everyone can be beautiful…and

SELF-RESPECT: THE SOLUTION TO UNSOLVABLE PROBLEMS

attractive. That translates into appearances. Appearances often supersede common sense. You don't need a cool car you can't afford. The reality is you won't have it very long. But it's attractive. That's the odd thing about life. Left alone it reconstitutes itself. It does it by attracting cooperative relationships. "There's a lid for every pot." the saying goes. There's Love for every sensibility. There's opportunity in every experience. It's in the way you express your priorities. What's important? Why? Who's it important to? Maybe it's not important at all. With self-respect you appreciate everything that makes you different and everything that makes you the same. Step away from the crowd and see what attracts you, not because someone else likes it but because it rings true to your soul. That's your motivation. It's that glimmer of satisfaction that leads you to it. Much of your life is spent following trends. That's how you accommodate everyone's free will and live peaceably in society. You follow the average. You follow the crowd. There are benefits to society you wouldn't want to miss. But you don't have to believe everything society tells you. Self-respect expects you to express your point of view. Creation won't ignore you, so do your best and be yourself.

You want to be the champion. It could be on stage at the Emmys or fantasizing the perfect romance. Every thought you have includes the impulse to succeed. You want to express yourself. You want to contribute to society and do what you like. But first you have to stay alive. Life is both independent and dependent. You have free will and you have life's necessities. Breathe. Eat. Drink. Procreate...Create. Those are your hungers. They motivate you to support yourself. Zoom to the future and your standing on Mars or singing at the Met. There's no in-between. Once you're stable, you want everything. It's like getting lost in the woods. You don't know where you are. Then you find the main road and everything makes sense. You need to know where you are. Life's confusing. It's mysterious and dangerous. You don't mind taking a risk, especially when others have done it before. But risking your life when nothing makes sense is terrifying. It's the predicament of mental illness. The mind doesn't operate in its normal patterns so it doesn't know what to do. Nothing's where it should be and you don't know where to look. The lines are blurred so it's impossible to know what to trust. Life must be reinvented to make sense. But how?

Choices mean something. Your prime motive is to make the right choice. You don't want to screw things up. You want to know you're headed in the right direction. You won't be perfect but it's important to know you did what you could. Life can't judge you. There are no valid comparisons. Life is excelling as you are. God doesn't care about obstacles. It cares about knowing itself. Don't make your problems into a science. Don't nitpick. You know how you feel. Question yourself and figure it out. Don't relive pains you don't have to. Feel God's purpose in your purpose. That feeling will draw you to it. It's the unlimited beauty of God's presence. It's the perfection of energy. Character projects your self-respect. If you don't question your character there's no reason to be here. You're not here to drink champagne till you can't stand up. You're here to put Love to work. You're here to find ways to feel the same unity God feels. Words can't describe it. It's the greatest feeling there is. Every thought you have is an attempt to align your character with God. The sensation of Love is just a taste of what God is. Still, it's more than enough to make it your life.

It's more than "success." It's how you feel about being successful. It's your *sense* of achievement. It's the freshness in feeling clean. It's your satisfaction when the parts fit perfectly. It's the right word at the right time. It's the solution. It's not an emotion. It's God's presence. It's God's perfection. It's the moment of unity. "Eureka. I've found it!" You've done it. Every moment is spent seeking that feeling. It's reconnecting what's become the illusion of individuality. It's the universal reunion. It's one thought that loves everything. That's what drives you. It's more than success. It's your relief that you're whole again. You're one with Creation.

That's the thrill. You get to explore your purpose. Self-respect fills in the gaps. It's your life's design. It's your "calling," your raison d'etre. God knows why, but it appeals to you. It's a thrill because the challenge never ends. It's a family business passed on to the next generation. It's the build-up to your dream vacation. It's all the opportunities you'll ever discover. Creation sees a good thing and moves it forward. That's what makes it fun. Rigid expectations are easily disappointed. An accountant doesn't have to work as an accountant. They can be a business person. It's a logical progression because the details are the same. It's simply a matter of who takes the risk. It's your trust the world will send you in the right direction. Your goal is to do better and enjoy the

SELF-RESPECT: THE SOLUTION TO UNSOLVABLE PROBLEMS

mystery of what "better" might be. Everything focuses on that thrill. It's the beauty in having a say in your destiny. Life goes on till you've had enough. Then everything goes back to the beginning. You evaluate and start again. Self-respect is a round-trip ticket. You teach God and God teaches you. You evolve so God can evolve.

Motivation begins the transformation. It's the frightened young soldier training to be an unstoppable fighter. It takes a liability and makes it an asset. Having a purpose is a blessing but most of us would like goals we don't have to work for. That's where your commitment comes in. It doesn't leave room for a doubt. It's a plan before a threat forces you to act unprepared. Training is a plan. Training is preparation. It's not a goal. It's your belief that you can accomplish any goal with the right training. So believe in your support. Encouragement helps but you still have to do it yourself. Be sure it's what you want. When you're new to a job you have to learn the skills that accomplish that job. And you have to learn not to make mistakes. Then you can do anything. But you're up against the wiliest creature in the Universe, a human being. Particularly, it's YOU! You want it to be easy. You want it to be fun. You want it to be interesting. Your mind wants you to be comfortable. But it's a two-edged sword. Avoidance is easy, but it doesn't accomplish anything. Change your mind. You're supposed to change your mind when you find a better way. Finding a better way is always your motive. A better way decides your approach to what you're doing. It's your desire for a bigger house or your need to fix a toothache. It's important so you plan for it. You learn what to do then direct yourself to do it. 80% of life is believing in yourself. 20% is doing it. 100% is meeting the challenge. Life's a chore. That's what your free will is for. From your soul's point of view life is different frequencies of energy. So you change your life by changing the frequencies like changing the channel on TV. It sounds weird but it's easy. You simply shift your attention. First you're watching a drama then you're watching a comedy. You re-evaluate the details from your new point of view. The world changes when you shift your attention. Problems disappear and secrets are revealed. New ideas inspire your consciousness. It creates a sense of comfort you're in charge. Then you can rely on your comfort to make your life better. There's plenty you're up against but you have choices. So do what makes you stronger. Your emotions tune in to all life's frequencies. Whether it's building a cabin in Alaska or raising a puppy, the trick is how you match yourself to the frequencies you like.

Unfortunately, you can overdo it and make a problem. You want to be motivated because you want to, not because you have to. You don't want a problem that leaves you with no choice. Addictions are like that. You can walk away from most problems even when the disappointment hurts terribly, like a failed romance or getting fired. You still have opportunities. While you have the choice to say "No." to an addiction, its nature makes it a problem. It's hard to do. Physically and mentally, it can tie you in knots. An addiction becomes stronger than your common sense. If you keep losing money gambling, then stop gambling. If drugs make you ignore taking care of yourself, then stop taking drugs. An addiction, instead of being a goal, becomes a compulsion. It's the Sirens' song from Greek mythology that's so alluring it draws the doomed sailors to crash on the rocks. It's a perverse motivation because it forces you to choose something that's bad for you over your own welfare. At first it seems manageable. But in time it becomes hopelessly compelling. Addictions are psychological problems that morph into physical problems; like debt, disease, and dysfunctional relationships. They own you. The original seduction becomes a command. You lose self-control and, with it, your self-respect.

Everyone's motivation is to feel good. Satisfaction is the ultimate motivation. It can be mountain climbing or a double bacon cheeseburger. It's your freedom to choose what Peace means to you. Then you evaluate where you are and try to do better. It's your evolution. It's your life. It's your values and priorities. It's what you're willing to do to have it. It's your accomplishments and stability. That's what your identity decides. Your free will makes it possible. Choose a role model, anyone you admire. Then copy them and match yourself to what you like about them. Once you have a goal, having a role model is a great second step. You simply adjust their attitude to fit your goal. For some it's a limousine. For others it's a hot dog cart. Or it could be a thousand hot dog carts. You want your life to please you. Whatever it is, it should be perfect. Self-respect is perfect. That's its attraction. Your Love reaches out and the Universe hands it back to you.

Your first lessons are from friends and family. They're your teachers. They're your role models. You mimic what they do. You want to be grown up.

SELF-RESPECT: THE SOLUTION TO UNSOLVABLE PROBLEMS

Grown-ups know how to do things. They know what's important. They have the freedom of their free will. They've learned self-respect. That should be your motive too. It can be a formal education or job experience. It loves something so much that you know everything about it. For your body, it's health. For your mind, it's wisdom. For your feelings, it's joy. And for your soul, it's Peace. It's whatever it is and as close as you can come to it. Once you know what you want, you have to find someone who knows how to do it so you can learn how. You have to see it from every angle because, in the end, it's about you. There's a particular angle you find attractive. You can't be someone else and expect it to last. That's imitation and you'll have no idea why you're doing it. You want to learn what your role model knows, but it has to be from your point of view. That's self-respect. Whatever you want has to be in harmony with who you are and who your soul wants you to be.

God knows you're perfect. Claiming your perfection is what motivates you. God sees beauty everywhere. That's why it's important to respect yourself no matter what. God won't give up on you. It'll never doubt you. It's always with you. It doesn't care what the world says. Sometimes you have to be an explorer. You won't have the same role models most people have. Few have been where you're going. It's not that people don't want to help. They just don't know what you need. They've never been exposed to it the same way you have. God knows and God will help you. And there are plenty of angels who'd love to get involved. Invite them in to be part of your life. Religion makes God your role model. It gives you a base to build your life on. All religions have the same purpose: to show you how to have a better life. There isn't one right way to love God. Just love God. It's not what you wear or the language you pray in. Your motive is to be whole with God. It's the reverence that shares God's momentum. Get there however you can but head in that direction. Peace is waiting for you and Peace is pushing you ahead.

Whatever the world needs and however you see it, Peace is what you want. Your self-respect just wants it at a fair price. Sail the Pacific or read a book, if it gives you Peace, it's perfect. And it's the thousands of changes you make to do it. It's your responsibility. Once you start, you're in to the end. But until it's over you can always win. So your motivation is to keep going! Success is your attitude to keep going despite the adversities. It's working through any environment; broken bones or broken hearts. Life will give you what you need. You already have the greatest cheerleader ever...God! So you can do it. Be realistic. Be honest. Be brave. *Be willing* to pay the price. Have no illusions. You'll meet life on life's terms. We all have to do it. You can't help someone who doesn't want help. You can't get someone to do something *for themselves* against their will. Choice is a matter of need. Someone may not want to improve their attitude, but they'll eat when they're hungry. The hardest thing is to change someone's attitude. Threats don't work. Rewards don't work. Interventions don't work. Self-respect is a monolith. The only thing that can change it is itself. All anyone can do is share their experience and hope someone appreciates it...that and a lot of Love.

Life is more than appearances. It's respecting yourself for who you are. Unless you respect yourself, whatever you achieve doesn't matter. After the exhilaration of winning, there's no real satisfaction in greed. It's a bottomless pit. Ambition is great as long as it's balanced by character. Character supports Love. You have to include yourself when you love Creation. If you want a good life, then respect Love. That's your motive whether you know it or not. Love supports everything. So care about everything. Your values are your interpretation of Love. Maturity is your responsibility guided by Love. Be generous. You can have a good reason to want something, but the world matters too. Its priorities must be respected. There's always something important to you. It might be a trendy t-shirt or overcoming paralysis. You decide the value and it doesn't have to make sense to anyone else. God has a dream for you. Don't give it up if all you need is patience. Enjoy your motivation and the world will be a willing partner.

You can be motivated or not. Motivation is an attitude. Like confidence, some people have it and some people have to learn it. It's useful because it gets things done. But you need priorities. They decide where you're going with it. Your soul is motivated or you wouldn't expose yourself to life's trials. Life's not easy. Anyone who wants anything needs to be motivated. You have to decide if it's worth it and accommodate the cost. You may have a long commute to a job that pays you well. If you want something you have to be an achiever regardless of the cost. Achievement is your motive. "The victor gets the spoils." So be a victor even if the prize is to sit in the sun and do nothing. It takes a lot of work to do nothing. Life will resist you. Energy without a purpose is wasted. Rest as much as you need, but have goals even as simple

SELF-RESPECT: THE SOLUTION TO UNSOLVABLE PROBLEMS

as making a list. One look at a homeless person is all it takes to see it. And you have to handle the boredom. You're either homeless looking for a way to feed yourself or rich with too much time on your hands. That's the joy of the middle class. They're comfortable and they keep busy working at it.

Self-respect is your motivation. Your success is God's motivation. You're motivated to explore your free will. It's your mandate for existence. It's how you help God understand its endlessness. You have free will and you have responsibilities. Self-respect joins them together. Like a momma bird, God urges you to spread your wings and fly. Self-respect, like flying, is your nature. God wants you to fly. It wants you to know justice, pride and purpose. It wants you to have Peace. It wants you to be free. Free will is the magic of Creation. It's where Eternity comes from. Free will is your contribution to God's evolution. It means that you're limitless. That's why God follows you so closely. It wants you to try new things. Even if you fail, you learned something God can use. Creation is God regenerating itself. You feel it. That feeling is your freedom to question every thought you have. Every day you're on the edge of an abyss then God pushes you over. Life's achievement is learning to trust yourself in freefall. God knows you can't fail. You and God are a team. If you thought about it for someone else you'd be in awe. That's what self-respect is. It's awe for yourself. It's awe for Creation that this all makes sense.

Motivation is your responsibility. You have to take the initiative. You have to do something. "Where there's a will, there's a way." It's an old proverb for being successful despite life's struggles. It's not a new, psychological technology. It's not a mental exercise. It's common sense. You have free will so use it. Direct it. Decide...or life will decide for you. Know what you want. Every atom in Creation is shouting to be heard. Your rightful place is to make your case for being here. You're entitled to your choices but you have to work at it. You have to let Creation know what you want. You have to trust you can do it no matter how confused you are. Your self-respect hands you the reins. The facts may confuse you. Your emotions may confuse you. Your lack of experience may confuse you. But with a clear head, your logic is intact and the physics doesn't change. So rely on Love. It's your nature. It's your connection to everything. Like the smell of fresh bread, Nature drives your hungers. Self-respect is your experience. It's your choice and you control it. It's your moral satisfaction, and it feels great when you honor it.

Don't miss out!

Visit the website below and you can sign up to receive emails whenever Martin Tomback publishes a new book. There's no charge and no obligation.

https://books2read.com/r/B-A-YBAKB-SYZIE

BOOKS 2 READ

Connecting independent readers to independent writers.

www.ingramcontent.com/pod-product-compliance
Lightning Source LLC
LaVergne TN
LVHW051056080426
835508LV00019B/1915

lifestyles. I envisioned myself managing a long-term care facility, making sure that older adults were provided with excellent skilled care services when they became incapacitated and their families were no longer able to take care of them.

Union's interdisciplinary approach to teaching and learning prepared me to engage in a variety of experiences in service and leadership that took me in a completely different direction. Because I was exposed to various disciplines that presented different approaches and perspectives, I was afforded many opportunities to expand beyond my original vision. During my Union journey I served as an administrator in a community foundation that provided grants to various non-profit organizations to improve the lives of many citizens in the Greater Cincinnati community. I was introduced to many community leaders who set a standard for leadership and service, and they became role models and coaches for me.

In the past nine years, I have been an administrator and educator in higher education, an area where I have found my passion. It is an awesome experience to interact with young multi-cultural college students who are just beginning their higher education journeys. I have watched them enter as first-year students who are unsure of themselves, yet excited about entering college. Within four years, they transform and graduate as mature, knowledgeable, young adults, still excited as they enter into professional careers. I continue to be of service to older adults living in long-term care facilities by being a volunteer ombudsman. In that capacity I advocate for older adults by making sure their rights and needs are met while living in these facilities. I am a board member of local organizations seeking to improve the health of African Americans in our community with breast cancer and HIV/AIDS. Where else could I have received the education that would allow me to serve in such diverse areas at the same time? Union Institute & University brought me to a place that I could not envision, and I am grateful and blessed to have had the opportunity to travel on the Union journey.

JUANITA S. TATE, Ph.D., 2006
Interdisciplinary Studies with a Concentration in Health Administration, Gerontology, Education
Director of Divisional Diversity Initiatives,
Miami University, Oxford, Ohio

The capacity to 'think out-of-the-box' is what I consider to be one of my finest professional assets. It enables me to look into a given situation and to find the possibilities, no matter how small or mounting the problem at hand may be. This is one of many attributes nurtured by my Union experience. When I decided to pursue a doctoral degree, I knew that I was embarking on a lifelong career as a 'servant leader'. I knew it was important that I attend a specific kind of university. I wanted to produce something of value for the world, something that would touch upon the lives of many people, that would contribute to the quality of life. I wanted to purse a course of study that would sponsor my independence, and one that would stretch not only my knowledge, but also my potential as a professional and as an entrepreneur. Union helped to instill in me a vision to see the pathways leading toward hope in a world teaming with fear and suffering, wonder and excitement. Union was a careful choice for me, and it has afforded me a powerful platform.

My purpose then and now is to discover ways to 'render spirit into everyday life'. At the root of most problems I encounter in the university classrooms where I teach or in the corporate boardrooms where I consult, are 'crises of consciousness'. The problems and challenges in my professional interventions continue to point to this. Therefore, I am moved to produce 'tools' and anecdotes to address the roots of consciousness and spirituality in the global society. Union's interdisciplinary model, academic rigor, and the 'green light' to go ahead and be passionate about my chosen specialization, served to fortify my strength and my will to step out and to pursue an inspired course of work, one that ultimately advances the common welfare.

On a personal level the value of lifelong learning, also a quality of the Union experience, is instilled as a guiding principle. I am grateful to have had the freedom to delve into spirituality and mysticism and, from an interdisciplinary standpoint, to have explored and established these in relationship to that which is practical and heuristic.

My work today is built upon a foundation that is at ease with taking risks, one that keeps me in balance and growing professionally and personally. It is a foundation that enables the work to evolve with the trends and the times. I draw great satisfaction from its legacy of service thus far and its continued promise. WISDOM TO GO is a product that my Union experience helped to shape and it is poised to serve the human community as we approach the threshold of a new era.

ELIZABETH D. TAYLOR, Ph.D., 1988
*Management and Organizational Development
with a concentration in Behavioral Sciences and Depth Psychology*
Founding President, WISDOM TO GO, Author

In the early 1960s, Loretto Heights College for Women in Denver was run by an order, The Sisters of Loretto, a progressive order of nuns. They were not overly pious or passive women, but feminists who convened consciousness-raising groups on campus and were the first nuns to discard the habit. While charting the changes among women's religious orders, the college president was meeting with other university presidents to realize a vision of the first university without walls. The first colloquium in the history of The Union Institute was held at Loretto Heights College the year that I was a freshman.

As fascinating as it was to witness these changes, I had no direction and quit school to get married after my Sophomore year so that my husband could get his degree. He was, after all, more likely to support us than I was, even if I earned a degree. I always regretted that decision and held fast to the conviction that I would finish some day. I worked in the travel industry for 20 years until I decided I needed to expand my horizons. I found a degree completion program and earned a B.A. in business management. When I was persuaded by a friend to apply for a master's program in social work, I no idea what a social worker actually did. Two years, five internships, 72 hours of course work, and 4 part time jobs later, I received an M.S.W. degree the year I turned 50.

The day after graduation I accepted a job as the clinical coordinator of a hospital adolescent addiction treatment program. A colleague who was completing her doctorate in education, while working at my hospital, told me that her program provided direction, limitless opportunity, and unflagging support, resulting in earning a Ph.D. and creating one's highest dream. She said the school had been around since the 60s.

I ordered the application packet and applied to the doctoral program that was about realizing one's dreams. My dream was to conduct research about having been a war-orphaned daughter. I wondered if other people whose fathers were killed in WW II felt as I did. One of the nuns from Loretto Heights, still my mentor, said she had earned her doctorate in art history from The Union Institute and knew it would be perfect for me.

When I presented my proposal on the last day of my Entry Colloquium in February 2000, I told my fellow learners that I wanted to find my father's lost crash site in Germany; to conduct a cross-cultural study with other women who had the same experience; to find a place for myself in psychology that embraced feminism; and to create a documentary film about my experience. Everyone cried as I showed them photos of my young father in his uniform.

As part of my program, I created an internship in Europe, the better to explore my research topic and to begin the search for my father's crash site. I completed peer days in Rome, Seattle, Phoenix, New Mexico, Arizona, and California. Two seminars were held in New Mexico, at Santa Fe and at Ghost Ranch in Abique. The third was in a yurt at a Zen retreat center in Sausalito. I did course work at Wellesley at the Jean Baker Miller Institute for Relational/Cultural Psychology (a feminist-based ideology), and I spent some time at Evergreen University in Olympia, Washington researching their collaborative learning model.

I made a number of lifetime friendships among peers as we served on various committees, met at seminars, and supported each other through our programs. There were no limits to what we could explore and experience. When I graduated two years after my colloquium, I had completed my study of women whose fathers had died in war. With a search team assembled in Germany, we were near discovery of my father's crash site. As a result, I found that I had created a new specialty in Grief and Loss. My Union doctoral program gave me the focus and the methods to conduct original research. We found my father's crash site in 2003, recovered his plane and his remains, and buried him in Arlington in October 2006. In addition, Der Spiegel Television produced a documentary film about my search and my father's last flight. My dream was realized and I had earned a Ph.D. in the process.

My degree from UI&U enables me to work as a tenured professor of psychology and social work as well as to serve as chair of Women's Studies at a university in Washington. I have published articles and made presentations about my P.D.E. research and have received many teaching awards. Our film has been distributed throughout Europe since 2005, and will have its premiere in the United States at the World War II Museum in New Orleans in August, 2010.

When I am asked about where I received my Ph.D., I give the following response, "From the original university without walls, created in the 60s for innovative learners who believe in possibility — it's a dream-realizing school." That's what I say and it's all true.

SHARON TAYLOR, Ph.D., 2002
Concentration in Relational Psychology

During my first residency at Union Institute & University, I proposed a project that took some convincing before it was approved: I would write a novel over the course of my four semesters. During each semester, I would address an aspect of the book, thus allowing me to explore new intellectual landscapes. Indeed, I often began semesters feeling as though I were headed into the desert without a compass, but I was always provided enough direction to find my bearings and then to discover the beauty of that desert, lonely as my personal educational travels could sometimes be.

Fortunately, I began by working with the gifted author, Matthew Goodman, and together, we worked on the actual writing of the novel. Matthew was quite astute in helping me choose the best novels to read for insights into how to conquer some of obstacles that had presented themselves. For one, I had a tendency to "run short" when writing; I rushed toward endings. Matthew taught me how to read as a writer and to address that and other issues by dissecting how different authors handled similar problems. I continue to read novels the same way, with one eye being that of an "ordinary reader" and the other that of a writer, always looking for why techniques work or fail.

The semester I spent under the tutelage of Cathy Stanton proved crucial. My novel entailed historical themes, and I therefore began what became a semester of investigating historiography. I rediscovered history, saw it in spectacular new light, which revealed that it was never as simple as any one book made it seem. I continue my reading in this subject, and I've never lost the sense that all history is perspective, that it cannot be simply objective no matter what the intent of the author.

Finally, I required a semester that in some way involved art. This semester proved crucial less to the novel that I was writing than to my next novel, which will be published in 2011. Working with digital imagery during that semester, I unwittingly provided myself enough background to begin researching how I might write a novel regarding September 11, 2001 from a cubist perspective. Rhoda Carroll, my instructor, also pushed me past my objections to writing poetry. I now publish poetry as often as I do short fiction.

The results of all this varied work were predictably unpredictable. I'm currently working as a full-time volunteer Public Relations Manager for SMART Recovery. I'm also pursuing an M.A. at Gonzaga University. Combining these two efforts, I hope one day to work in a public relations' capacity for a nonprofit organization. Meanwhile, my writing continues, as wonderfully unpredictable as was my education at Union Institute.

PAUL A. TOTH, Ph.D., 1996
Concentration in Psychoanalysis

I first learned about the Union from psychologist Carl Rogers, at a program sponsored by his Center for the Studies of the Person in La Jolla, California. It was the summer of 1971 and I was a Catholic priest working as a Campus Minister at Drake University in Des Moines. The discussion was about graduate programs, and Carl said that he thought the recently formed Union was the most creative option of which he was aware.

A few years later, I decided to take a sabbatical and do some graduate studies in counseling to enhance my work with students and faculty. I had a hard time finding out how to get a hold of the Union but finally located it in Yellow Springs, Ohio. My application was provisional as I was still priest and there was some concern about whether I would fit in with the Union program of multidisciplinary studies. I traveled to Yellow Springs and met with Roy Fairfield and won his approval. (It was probably the plaid pant suit and my beard that convinced him).

Through the support of a friend I applied to the Danforth Foundation and presented them with a plan to study psychotherapy and human sexuality. I was given enough money to fund my participation in various workshops at the Esalen Institute, the Institute for the Study of Human Sexuality, the Masters and Johnson Institute in St Louis, and the Kinsey Institute at Indiana University. These were the foremost programs dealing with the nascent study of the subject.

Being a priest I knew that my knowledge about sex was minimal. But I found that people were happy to meet a priest who was interested in the subject. As I would discover years later, this was also the period when the major experiences of clergy abuse were taking place. The Union helped me to discover my own sexual self without taking advantage of young people, as well as to explore the burgeoning knowledge about sexuality.

I worked with a committee of local people along with my U.G.S. mentor, a former nun and in September of 1978, I completed my program (my Terminar). I had started a private practice in Fall of 1975 with two psychologists. Thanks to the support of my Bishop I continued my work in my office until I decided that I needed to leave the priesthood. At about that time I met the woman who would become my wife. We were together for twelve years and had one son.

I have continued in private practice, and am now semi-retired, but I continue to see clients each week to help them with their sexual issues. The Union was very valuable to me as it enabled me to receive excellent multi-disciplinary education in a field that was just beginning to develop. At the time of my learning project, there was no doctoral level program in sexuality therapy.

I have held adjunct positions teaching graduate students at the University of Iowa School of Social Work and Des Moines University (training medical students). Thus I have been able to mentor others thru my own specialized learning program. I am very grateful to the Union for the opportunities it has given me.

T. николаs Tormey, Ph.D., 1978
Counseling and Human Sexuality

*I*nterviewing school administrators in China, exploring the land that Georgia O'Keefe painted, serving an internship for a welfare-to-work agency and completing a dissertation on a topic about which I was passionate were a few of the very significant and authentic pieces of my Union program. Where else can such authenticity in education be found? These experiences were just a sample of my three year journey of self-directed study in an intense mentor-based program, one that eventually led to the completion of my doctorate in Interdisciplinary Studies with a concentration in the Cultural Foundations of Education, awarded in 2004.

I was in the final years of my career in public education as teacher and administrator, when I was accepted into the doctoral program at Union. The experiences of guiding my own academic journey under the close tutelage of Dr. Cynthia L. Jackson, who provided the most valuable instruction in researching and writing a dissertation that one could ever have, resulted in my fulfilling my lifetime career goal of teaching at the university level.

Following my public school career and the completion of my doctorate, I served as an adjunct assistant professor at LeMoyne College in Syracuse, New York, the State University of New York at Oswego, at Alfred State College, Alfred, New York. These positions eventually led to a full-time visiting professor position at Alfred University where I was able to integrate the information and knowledge from my Union academic experience with my own real-life field experiences as I instructed future teachers. Experiencing the interdisciplinary content of Union's program prepared me well for the writing of my own course syllabi, choosing textbooks, and developing new course proposals.

Another important aspect of my Union program was the rich friendships that I discovered from Alaska to Hawaii and many places in between. These friendships, I have no doubt, will be lifelong and have brought some wonderful opportunities. Most recently, my wife and I returned to the classroom to teach 23 Middle School girls at Clearview Christian Girls School, in Maui, which is owned and operated by close friend and Union Alum, Dr. Vicki Drager. We donated our time and energy in exchange for a place to live and a car to drive. What a marvelous connection and experience!

Successfully completing this doctoral journey required the help and assistance of many. No one completes this degree alone. I know that without the support and encouragement of my family, wife Carolyn, daughter Bethany, my mother Irene Trombly, my Core Advisor Dr. Cynthia L. Jackson, my committee members and my colloquium colleagues, I would not have completed this powerful, authentic academic journey. And to special friend and Union alum Dr. Steven

Swerdfeger, who introduced me to the Union program, I remain forever indebted.

GREGORY D. TROMBLY, Ph.D., 2004
Interdisciplinary Studies, with a concentration in the Cultural Foundations of Education

In 1968, my civil rights activities in the Oakland, California Mexican American community took a significant turn when I chose to accept a position as EEO Investigator with a new federal civil rights agency, the U.S. Equal Employment Opportunity Commission (EEOC). As a Chicano activist, among other things, I had edited a monthly newspaper, the Oakland Mexican American Political Association Newsletter (MAPA), which documented MAPA activities; they included voter registration drives, political campaigns, protesting job, education, and housing discrimination, protesting police brutality, and conducting public demonstrations for equal opportunity. I was named the Viva Bobby Kennedy for President County Chairman.

In 1969, with no prior formal academic training, I enrolled in evening classes at San Francisco Law School. In 1971, before I completed my legal training, I accepted an appointment as District Director of the new Phoenix, Arizona, Office of EEOC. In 1974, I was accepted as a doctoral student in the Union Graduate School Program and have been in a state of accelerated transformation ever since. From the very first colloquium, I experienced a new world of thought, understanding, exploration, and engagement. I learned the inextricable linkage between vision, direction, and achievement. I developed a comprehensive understanding of the innovative models for inclusion in national civil rights imperatives. The interdisciplinary spirit, along with public policy inquiry concepts provided by UGS, helped me become an agent of social change. I began to document experiences, which would have historic cultural and political implications on the Hispanic community. Stanford University Library has kindly accepted the Dr. Edward Valenzuela Papers in their Special Collections Branch. I founded and became National President of a national Hispanic government employees Association, IMAGE, which included 125 chapters in 40 states. I was called to White House meetings and have met with Congressional leaders. I also authored a book on Immigration and another entitled *Expand Your Mind Power*. I became the Dean of the Hispanic Leadership Institute, professor of leadership studies, and also taught graduate level courses; I conducted leadership training at the Houston Space Center with Astronaut Franklin Chang Diaz for NASA.

At EEOC, before retiring in 1988, I was involved in the investigation of over 50,000 case of job discrimination. During years of struggles I had focused on attempts to improve the participation of Hispanics in government, which was documented in my 1977 UGS Dissertation "The Spanish Speaking and Government Employment." The last chapter of this document constituted an employment plan for the systematic hiring of Hispanics into the Jimmy Carter Administration. But, the Federal Employment System is a tough nut to crack! After forty years of struggle, we find that Latinos are still the only minority group under-represented in federal jobs in proportion to their participation in the civilian labor force! Today, in part because of my UGS experience, I am participating in meetings in the Obama White House to address this crisis through a proposal called "a Call to Action."

Ed Valenzuela, Ph.D., 1977
Socio-Political Economy
Co-Chair, National Coalition for Fairness of Hispanics in Government
Executive Director, Arizona Fair Housing Center

My Union Journey began in 2001 and was completed in 2006. I am currently the President of Diablo Valley College (DVC) in Pleasant Hill, California. We serve approximately 32,000 students per year and are one of California's 110 public community colleges. I was previously President of Berkeley City College (BCC) from 2004-2007, another California public community college, where I was fortunate in getting to provide the leadership for completing a six story, single facility urban campus. This nearly $70,000,000 project resulted in a LEED silver certification and was the first permanent site for BCC, which was over 30 years old.

My leadership quest at Union began with an opportunity to reflect on my own strengths through the seminars and peer days. Because I had spent several years working as a mid-level bureaucrat in higher education, I wanted a program that would allow me the opportunity to explore the depth and breadth of humanistic principles and apply them to leadership in an educational institution. California's community colleges are the actualization of one of the finest social public policies ever crafted; any person can attend a California community college.

Leadership can be understood in many ways and in my studies I was able to connect with poets, philosophers, economists, organizational development gurus, scientists and many other writers through my advisor, Robert Atkins, who spent many hours walking with me through all the possibilities that emerged throughout my internship and course work.

DVC has endured accreditation issues, organizational issues, a $46,000,000 construction project in the center of campus, and the worst budget year that California has ever experienced. I learned that Leadership is not only an art, but also the ability to hold the space to allow the organism to transform itself. Union gave me the language to describe what I tentatively had been practicing but had not been able to articulate. I learned how to identify core strengths of base values, which will provide the basis for organizational renewal and development. Using wisdom from past experiences we can see patterns and envision the future in this global society. Union gave me, a first generation college student, the opportunity to become a college president.

JUDY E. WALTERS, Ph.D., 2006
Specialization in Leadership & Organizational Effectiveness

One week after Hurricane Katrina devastated New Orleans, I was peering at the morass of flotsam cascading through the streets and shaking my head in disbelief. Even though I had seen hours and hours of television coverage of the disaster, nothing had prepared me for this demonic horror. Water and debris covered what I remembered as one of America's most fun places to visit. Within a few months, we opened the UEP Gulf Coast office in a building still undergoing renovation. We announced to the world that we were open for business and ready to help the many devastated small businesses that called New Orleans home. Most had lost everything in the flood and needed help in reconstructing their businesses and, more importantly, becoming viable and profitable. With financial support from the Kauffman Foundation as well as the White House Economic Advisors, political leaders and nonprofit leaders, I helped conceive, develop and implement the UEP/UEP Gulf Coast, which provided a lifeline to these small businesses.

In April 2009, I landed at Wayne County Airport on the way to meet with members of the New Economy Initiative, a program launched by ten major foundations in Detroit to rescue and resuscitate Detroit's industrial sector. The automobile industry as we knew it had been dead for some time, but the major automobile manufacturers refused to acknowledge it. The whole industry and those dependent on it were suffering. I was part of a team to help design, develop and implement a program to assist minority auto suppliers in Detroit to retool, reimagine and restructure their businesses to take advantage of new market opportunities in aerospace, healthcare, alternative energy and transportation. What was required was a new way of thinking and understanding of seemingly disparate parts. The UEP appeared to fit the bill perfectly.

If there was one thing I had learned at The Union Institute during my doctoral sojourn, it was the value of an interdisciplinary approach. From my initial Colloquium and Peer Days, to my Seminars and my dissertation, the interdisciplinary approach was underscored and inculcated in all of us. New learning was *de rigueur*, social awareness was critical and contributing to the body of knowledge was our *raison d'être*. My hope, indeed my prayer, is that the efforts we undertake in cataclysmic situations like New Orleans, Baton Rouge and Detroit will help advance the body of knowledge and success in improving the viability of small businesses. Moreover, it will signal that I have earned the right to be called a Union Graduate and have lived up to the ideals of this unique institution.

CHARLES ALEXANDER WEST, Ph.D., 2000
Entrepreneurship
President Dynamic Functions Consulting Group, Inc.

During my opening colloquium at Union, in the summer of 1997, one of the conveners challenged me to do what I loved most in pursuing my doctoral degree. In response to that challenge I studied spirituality, in particular the personal transformation required on the journey to becoming a spiritually mature adult. In my dissertation, I asked 90 Sisters of Charity to share with me their stories of faith, crisis and spiritual growth. I learned that God uses the ordinary events of life as a sacred container and engages all of us as agents of transformation in one another's lives — whether we know it or not. Quite naturally, I looked at my own life and wondered what lay ahead for me. How would I put into practice my interdisciplinary, socially relevant degree? Since my graduation I have taught at the college level, continued my scholarly research and worked as a development officer, but my Union journey took me halfway across the world as well.

I finished my Union requirements in the summer of 2000 just as my college-age son David was returning from a volunteer experience with the poor of the island nation of Madagascar. He told me about his work in the urban slums and rural villages of Tamatave, about the lack of sanitation, the malnutrition, the illiteracy. He told me about the remarkable religious brother from India with whom he had worked, a genius in the area of development who had great energy but few resources. The conversations around our kitchen table became my sacred container and David, an agent of transformation in my life. Our family created Caring Response Madagascar Foundation, a public charity that serves the poor of Madagascar. I put my research and writing skills to work as a grant writer designing projects that offered literacy, sanitation and financial opportunities to poor women and their families. The books in our literacy centers teach lifesaving skills about the importance of hand-washing and the use of the latrine. Our micro lending project provides courses in budgeting, nutrition and animal husbandry as requirements for receiving loans for chickens and cows. Interdisciplinary? You bet. Socially relevant? Absolutely.

Today I serve — as I have from its inception — as the volunteer director of Caring Response Madagascar Foundation. David serves as CRMF's president. To date, CRMF has brought nearly $1 million in grants, programs, supplies and services to the poor of Tamatave. It has become an agent of transformation in the everyday lives of people in

Madagascar. What a perfect sequel to my doctoral studies! I am infinitely grateful for my Union experience and for a graduate program that challenged me to ask: "How will you use your degree to serve?"

VIRGINIA RUEHLMANN WILTSE, Ph.D., 2000
Spirituality

Virginia Wiltse, Ph.D., also currently serves on the Board of Trustees of Union Institute & University

Achieving my doctorate from The Union Institute was more than "completing my education" as my colleagues thought of it. It was a bridge to what has become a life-long process of learning about the body and how to work with it. The "somatic" movement was relatively new in the late 1980s, but the idea of working with instead of on a client appealed to me. UI helped me build a philosophical (as well as practical) approach to helping people use their bodies well for a lifetime. And I was bridging careers from many years of university teaching to working one-to-one in a small company of my own creation. Now I have been drawn back into teaching to educate other practitioners in my holistic approach and I now teach internationally.

My company is Body-in-Motion (body-in-motion.com), through which I provide my training and teaching services as well as mentoring of other therapists. I have become a leader in developing manual techniques and preventative skills that every person can use to remain mobile and well long as he or she wishes to do so. These techniques address the fascia or connective tissue, the most ubiquitous material in the human body, which is at the root of most musculoskeletal pain. In 2007, the first International Conference on Fascia Research at Harvard officially opened the door to an inquiry that practitioners and scientists had been immersed in for years. The scientific literature grows daily on the importance of this soft tissue that used to be thought of as nearly inert, fibrous material.

I have also become a leader in the exercise field by creating solutions for body movement recovery unavailable in the conventional framework of the "gym." I used my understanding of the work of Rudolf Laban, Irmgard Bartenieff and Dr. Vladimir Janda, the late Czech psychiatrist, to create a functional exercise approach that honors the body in its innate and intrinsic patterns of movement. Work at the Chronic Pain and Stress Centre in Victoria, B.C., where I was mentored by Dr. Michael Greenwood also helped fashion my approach to treatment. Useful for all ages and fitness levels, my exercise approach, "3-D Workout™, documented on DVDs, provides the connectors, mobilizers and patterns that restore and maintain the body's basic organizational framework for standing and moving on two feet. I am proud to be of service to my colleagues, students and clients in the endlessly creative process of finding solutions for pain and mobility problems.

DIANNE L. WOODRUFF, Ph.D., 1992
Somatic Education

The Union is visionary. I first heard of it in the 1970s when it was The Union Institute of Experimenting Colleges and Universities. Unprecedented, unaccredited and untested, it offered creative thinkers a challenging opportunity to transform a desire to learn and to become an agent of change through an interdisciplinary "Learners Program" with the learner in charge. What a wild vision!

Then, serendipitously, my life in Hawai'i began to include people whom I admired who had their Ph.D.s from The Union: Peter Adler, Ellen Colburn, Mitzi Simonelli and Elizabeth Ayson. They all had two things in common: vision and careers that were soaring.

It took me seven years from my first Learners' Colloquium in 1982 until January 1989 to complete my doctoral program. Not in my wildest dreams could I have predicted that six years later I would receive

The Union's President's Award for Humanitarian Service.

The Union experience had affirmed my vision and given me wings.

In 1990 I was elected to the Hawai'ian House of Representatives. In my second term, I became Vice-Speaker of the House, the first woman ever to hold that position. My legislative record focused on civil rights as well as educational and environmental issues. In the mid 1990s I served as an executive member of DACOWITS (Defense Advisory Committee for Women in the Services), visiting military bases in Europe and Asia, while advising the U.S. Secretary of Defense on gender integration issues.

Many local and national awards have marked my career path.

But it wasn't always that way.

Before Union, I was a homemaker, raising four children in a military family that moved 14 times in a 23-year period.

During the first half of my life I was like a "spectator" witnessing mass discrimination and injustice: watching Pearl Harbor as it was bombed and Japanese families interned in camps; living in Berlin in 1961 and seeing East Berliners escaping communism before The Wall went up; and then residing in the south in 1962 before the Civil Rights Movement.

It was in the 1960s, when The Union was being founded, that I began to actively resume my education, looking for opportunities to learn and grow.

Since Union, during the second half of my life, I have endeavored to live as an "advocate" for social and economic justice issues.

In 1998, I was diagnosed with breast cancer and speak openly and publicly about my cancer experience. While the disease does not discriminate, there are disparities and minorities suffer an unequal burden of cancer.

Today, at 76 years of age, I am the Chief Staff Officer for Mission at the American Cancer Society Hawaii Pacific.

Yeats wrote that, "Education is not the filling of a pail but the lighting of a fire."

Thank you, Union Institute, for lighting my way.

JACQUELINE (JACKIE) YOUNG, Ph.D., 1982
Concentration in Communications
Member of the Hawai'i State Advisory Committee for the
U.S. Commission on Civil Rights, the Hawai'i Council on Economic Education
and founder and 17 year board member of Hale Ola,
a domestic violence community shelter.

I wrote most of my Project Demonstrating Excellence with the inspiration of dawn breaking over the Himalayas as seen out my window. It was the mid-1980s and I had already been living in Kathmandu for several years. I had, by then, a master's degree in Public Health from a mainstream university in the United States, a job at a startup think tank run by senior Nepali intellectuals, a garment business that included two boutiques, a small export arm, and a workshop that I was trying hard to staff with women, and a three-year-old son who I was co-parenting with my ex who lived on the other side of the Valley. Yes, I was busy, but I knew I wanted the advanced degree. I knew that I wanted to study. And I knew that for me action, learning and relevance were inseparable. I don't even remember how I found Union in those pre-internet days, but when I found it, it felt like an immediate fit.

It all came together when I bought the garment business from a lively Gurung women who was going overseas with her military husband. Although ultimately the business failed (I was neither a dress designer nor, as it turned out, a savvy entrepreneur), and the introduction of U.S. garment quotas quickly sucked up all of the skilled cutters in 100 mile radius of Kathmandu, it gave me a sobering perspective on how difficult it was to be a small entrepreneur in this country. It also made me wonder why, from among the many castes and ethnic groups that comprise modern day Nepal, some dominated the business landscape.

So I set out to investigate. I talked to hundreds of small manufacturers and traders in the plains, towns and hills of Nepal. In the course of these interviews, I also got an earful about government policies and practices. My P.D.E., which documented and analyzed what I heard and what I learned, was later published by Oxford University Press as well as briefly banned in Nepal.

Union was geographically far away during all of my doctoral process, but the moment I stepped into the first seminar, I felt a kinship with the peers and professors who had found their way there, too. Even in those pre-email days, the support and guidance of my committee and the knowledge that there were others pursuing their own life interests in a shared, spacious academic arena kept me on track. A small group of learners even came to me — for a one-week seminar that I helped to organize — around the cultures and development of Nepal.

Countries, continents, marriages, another child, and my own small consulting business later, I look back on the learning process and the Union experience, as a highlight of my life's journey.

LAURIE ZIVETZ, Ph.D., 1987
Social Economics
International Development Consultant

Union Institute & University offers undergraduate, masters, and doctoral programs that engage, enlighten, and empower individuals in their pursuit of a lifetime of learning and service.

UNDERGRADUATE PROGRAMS

Bachelor of Arts

Liberal Arts major with a variety of concentrations, offered online, or through brief residencies at our Vermont Centers in Montpelier and Brattleboro.

Bachelor of Science

Offering a variety of majors from Business, Education, and Social Work, to Criminal Justice, Psychology, and Emergency Services Management through low residency programs at our academic centers in Cincinnati, Los Angeles, North Miami Beach, and Sacramento.

MASTERS PROGRAMS

Master of Arts Online

Concentrations in Creativity Studies; Health and Wellness; History and Culture; Leadership, Public Policy, and Social Issues; Literature and Writing; Psychology; Education offered completely online with close mentoring from faculty and peers

Master of Arts with concentrations in Psychology and Counseling. Offered via brief residencies from our Brattleboro, VT Center.

Master of Education

Offered through our Vermont or North Miami Beach centers, or completely online.

DOCTORAL PROGRAMS

Ph.D. in Interdisciplinary Studies

Offered through brief residencies in Cincinnati, OH with concentrations in Ethical and Creative Leadership; Public Policy and Social Issues; Humanities and Society

Doctor of Psychology in Clinical Psychology (Psy.D.)

Offered through brief academic meetings in Cincinnati or Brattleboro, VT

Doctor of Education (Ed.D.)

Offered through brief residencies in Cincinnati.

www.myunion.edu

www.ingramcontent.com/pod-product-compliance
Lightning Source LLC
LaVergne TN
LVHW011420080426
835512LV00005B/164